T0209357

ENDORSEMENTS

"In sports and in life, we place so much emphasis on winning and losing; on being in the right place at the right time; on making decisions that impact life. Joe Bill Campbell has written an exceptional Christian devotional for young athletes, young adults and for anyone seeking THE TRUTH, THE WAY, THE LIFE. As the parents of young athletes and young adults, we highly recommend this book to anyone seeking to win The Game of Life-- through the acceptance of Jesus Christ as Lord and Savior. It is, indeed, a GAME CHANGER!".

-Jim and Juli Boeheim
A Syracuse University Basketball Family

"As a mother, step-mother and grandmother, I find the content of this faith-based series of devotionals very useful as a vehicle to talk with our young adult and teenage family members. Sometimes, you need a conversation-starter to have those meaningful discussions on subjects that are difficult to approach. This book does that job in an authentic, transparent way that aligns with Christian values and beliefs. It's an interactive method of storytelling and lesson learning."

-Henrietta Pepper, author of *Out of the Gate: What inspires us drives us forward.*, GCJ Consultants, LLC, a Brand Communications firm, Founder & Owner.

I have known Joe Bill Campbell all of my life. He has become a man devoted to Jesus. In his devotional book "Just Win, Baby", Campbell has reminded us that the central focus of winning is found in having a relationship with Jesus Christ. As 1 John 5:5 states, "Who is it that overcomes the world? Only the one who believes that Jesus is the Son of God". This devotional directs all of us to move past mere participation and to embrace the ultimate win in Jesus Christ. Joe Bill reminds us that victories on the field will be temporary, but the victory found in faith will be forever.

-Dr. Stephen L. Ayers
Lead Pastor
Hillvue Heights Church
Bowling Green, KY

"As a recently graduated student athlete of Syracuse University, I understand the importance of keeping your faith as your focus in college. With endless temptations and distractions, it is imperative to be involved in a church or some form of fellowship. For my teammates and me, it was regularly attending meetings at Fellowship of Christian Athletes at Syracuse. Joe Bill competed and was victorious at the highest level, both in sports and in the game of life. There was no secret to how he did it. It was through his Christian faith, coupled with his core values of hard work, grit, and determination. Just Win Baby compiles some of the most important scripture passages to know and memorize, as well as Joe Bill's advice from his own personal experiences. A true game changer!"

-Nick Giancola
Syracuse University B.S., M.S., Basketball Player, FCA Member

JUST WIN BABY:
The Game of Life

101
Game Changing
Christian Devotionals
for
Young Athletes/Young Adults

JOE BILL CAMPBELL

WESTBOW
P R E S S®
A DIVISION OF THOMAS NELSON
& ZONDERVAN

WestBow Press books may be ordered through booksellers or by contacting:

WestBow Press
A Division of Thomas Nelson & Zondervan
1663 Liberty Drive
Bloomington, IN 47403
www.westbowpress.com
844-714-3454

ISBN: 979-8-3850-0634-2 (sc)
ISBN: 979-8-3850-0635-9 (hc)
ISBN: 979-8-3850-0636-6 (e)

Library of Congress Control Number: 2023916403

Print information available on the last page.

WestBow Press rev. date: 11/7/2023

FOREWORD

In life, we are all fortunate if we have a few close friends who support us mentally, emotionally and spiritually. Joe Bill Campbell and I formed such a friendship during the 1980s. During my toughest times, he was there for me as my attorney and even more so as my friend. During his toughest times, I extended the same friendship to him. I was honored when he asked me to write this FOREWORD for his devotional: Just Win, Baby: The Game of Life. Joe Bill is genuine in his faith, lives by the Golden Rule, and has spent his life trying to make life better for others.

American culture has many parts, but none more absorbing than sports and religion. In my home state of Kentucky, it has frequently been said that basketball is a religion. During my tenure as a college and professional coach, I have found that fans are the same, no matter where you go. They love their teams, support their players, praise coaches who are victorious and criticize coaches who are not. Most all players, coaches and fans seek peace through their religious faith. As a Christian, I have been duly blessed with a beautiful family, a successful basketball career, but most of all, with knowing Jesus Christ as my Lord and Savior.

I am pleased to recommend Joe Bill Campbell's devotional not only to young athletes/young adults but to anyone seeking The Truth, The Way, The Life. I marvel at Joe Bill's effort to publish a Christian devotional at age 80. His correlation of Bible verses and sports expressions/metaphors is unique. He has not only captured the essence of sports but has found Bible verses that form a foundation for Christian living and for eternal victory. Young athletes, young adults, parents, and grandparents all need a foundation upon which to build a successful and enjoyable life, and which will lead to life eternally. Winning the Game of Life through acceptance of Jesus Christ as Lord and Savior provides just such a foundation.

As the father of two beautiful young athletes (Justine and Zachary - soon to be young adults), as the husband of my lovely wife, Brenda, and as a Christian, I embrace the message of the devotional: Just Win Baby: The

Game of Life. In life, you will haves wins and losses, but in Jesus Christ you will always have victory, peace, reassurance and best of all—Salvation.

Dwane Casey
Former NBA Head Coach (Timberwolves, Raptors, Pistons)
Former Assistant NBA Coach (Supersonics, Mavericks)
College Assistant (Western Kentucky University, University of Kentucky)

INTRODUCTION

Jesus Christ changes lives. He not only provides you with a better quality of life, but He is the only way to win the Game of Life, thus securing eternal life in Heaven. Jesus Christ changed my life, not once but twice. I accepted Him as my Savior at age 18. I knew the very moment I was saved. I continued with my education and career and along the way was the recipient of many of His blessings. I must admit, however, that though I knew Him as Savior, I had not yet made him the LORD of my life. At age 55, I experienced divorce, financial difficulty, the loss of both parents in the same year. I was at the lowest place in my life. Broke, depressed, not knowing what to do, I discussed my feelings with my ex-wife (who to this day is my very best friend). She gifted me a LIFE APPLICATION STUDY BIBLE, NEW INTERNATIONAL VERSION by Zondervan/Tynedale Publishing. I read the New Testament three times. I read most of the Old Testament. I studied the notes. I prayed and asked the Lord to help me. I made Him the LORD of my life and surrendered my will to His. He responded beautifully and abundantly. He restored my finances. He removed my sense of pride, my fear of failure. He blessed me physically, mentally, emotionally, and especially spiritually. How could I die and not share this experience with others? I remembered attending a seminar where a Christian lawyer posed the following question: "If being a Christian is a crime, is there enough evidence to convict you"? This resonated with me, and I began to search for a way to help others know Jesus Christ as Lord and Savior.

I found the answer in my grandchildren, Greer, Campbell, Turner, ages 10, 8, 4, respectively. The children of my daughter, Anne, and her husband, Lt. Colonel Jon Hawkins (US Army), provided the motivation to write a devotional that would impact their lives, the lives of their grandchildren, and hopefully the lives of young people everywhere for generations to come.

In high school, I lettered in four (4) sports: football, basketball, baseball and track. To this day, I am the only quarterback from my high school to be named first team all-state (United Press Team). I accepted a football scholarship to the University of Kentucky where I played one year under a Christian coach, Blanton Collier. Coach Collier was terminated after my first year. I transferred to my hometown university, Western Kentucky University ("WKU"), where I played two years. My first year at WKU we went undefeated (WKU's only undefeated football team) and won the Tangerine Bowl. The team was inducted into WKU's Team Hall of Fame.

As a result of my athletic endeavors, I have remained a lifelong fan of athletics. In thinking and praying about writing a devotional, I relied on my experiences as an athlete, as a sports fan, as a lawyer, but mostly on my personal relationship with Jesus Christ. Every word of my devotional is inspired by the Lord. I am not a minister, a preacher, a writer, or a teacher. I am a Christian committed to living in accordance with God's will for my life. My experience has been that society puts athletes on a pedestal. Successful athletes are perceived as leaders. Athletes can influence others and have a choice as to how to impact the lives of others. When athletes use their platform to praise and glorify Jesus Christ, it has a profound impact upon their peers and upon their audience. I wanted to write a devotional that would be particularly appealing to young people. Between ages 13 and 19, young people become subjected to peer pressure greater than at any other point in their lives. They have begun the search for their own identity. A devotional that reaches out to such a young group of athletes and young people will hopefully strengthen their relationship with Jesus Christ. It will allow them to resist sinful temptations, and to help others find the Lord. It was a 17-year-old teammate of mine who stood before the student body at a high school convocation and professed his faith in Jesus Christ that led me (and others) to the foot of the Cross where we accepted Christ as Savior. I want young people to know and experience the richness and fullness of life as a Christian by making Jesus the Lord of their lives, and to share their experience with their peers. I want to provide the support group (parents, grandparents, siblings and others) for young people with a unifying message that will profoundly impact the single most important decision anyone will make during their lives – whether to accept Jesus Christ as Lord and Savior.

The devotional is written simply, directly and redundantly. I learned from the Billy Graham ministry not to stray from the message. The core message in the devotional is John 3: 16 and John 3:17: accept Christ as Savior; make Him the Lord of your life; subjugate your will to God's will; share your blessings with others; be a giver, not a taker; be a servant to others; be active in sharing your faith with your peers; be more concerned with pleasing God than pleasing people. The Bible verses at the beginning of the devotional bring a biblical view to the sports metaphor/expression. Sports expressions and metaphors are so very pertinent to everyday life. The objective is to find expressions that relate to life and to weave them together with Bible verses that guide us on our life's journey. Each devotional has a GAME OF LIFE component wherein it explains how the Biblical verse and the sports expression go hand in hand in the Game of Life. Every Human being experiences the Game of Life. When it comes down to determining whether you have won or lost the Game of Life, the only decision that matters is whether you accepted Jesus Christ as Lord and Savior.

In preparing this devotional my hope, my purpose, my motivation can be succinctly stated as follows:

1. To bring praise and glory to Jesus Christ.
2. To leave my grandchildren, their grandchildren and young men/ women everywhere, an understanding of God's greatest blessing: Salvation through Jesus Christ.
3. To leave enough evidence so that my family, friends, and peers would "convict" me of being a Christian.

May God bless all who read this, and may young people everywhere run the race to the Cross where victory will be found in Jesus Christ.

ABOUT THE AUTHOR

Let me introduce myself. My name is Joe Bill Campbell. I am a lifelong resident of Bowling Green, Kentucky. I graduated from WESTERN KENTUCKY UNIVERSITY with a BA degree in English. I received my Juris Doctor law degree (with honors) from the University of Kentucky College of Law. After practicing law for more than 50 years, I retired in 2020. As a trial lawyer, I tried voluminous cases, mostly in the area of medical negligence and business litigation. I also represented several NCAA coaches in infraction cases. I was selected as a Fellow in the American College of Trial Lawyers. This organization selects and accepts only the top one percent (1%) of trial lawyers in each state for fellowship. I was the recipient of the Kentucky Bar Association's ("KBA") Most Outstanding Lawyer award. I was chosen as one of the top 50 lawyers in the Commonwealth of Kentucky by SUPERLAWYERS. I served as a member of the KBA's Board of Governors and as KBA President. I lead the Bar in creating LAWYERS MUTUAL INSURANCE COMPANY OF KENTUCKY, INC., a captive insurance company, insuring Kentucky lawyers for professional liability. I served as Chair of LMICK for approximately 15 years. In 2011, I was inducted into the University of Kentucky College of Law HALL OF FAME. I have served in leadership positions at both WKU (Chair, Board of Regents) and THE KENTUCKY COUNCIL ON HIGHER EDUCATION (Chair for 3 years). I have a passion for education which I consider a key to producing a better-quality life. It is with this passion that I decided to write this devotional – to educate young men/women on the importance of knowing Jesus Christ as Lord and Savior.

Joe Bill Campbell

DEDICATION

This Devotional is dedicated to the following:

TO MY LORD AND SAVIOR JESUS CHRIST:
Thank you for your amazing Grace which saved a wretch like me.

TO MY GRANDCHILDREN, GREER, CAMPBELL AND TURNER:
Your love inspired me to author this devotional so that not only will you have something to remember me buy, but also a guide for your life's journey.

TO MY CHILDREN, CLAY AND ANNE:
God chose me to be your father—a great blessing! Your love and support made me a better person, a better father, a better Christian. I love you.

TO MY SON-IN-LAW, LT. COLONEL JON HAWKINS:
Though I was never in the military, I would always want you in my "foxhole". Thank you for being a great friend and for your 20 plus years' service in the United States Army.

TO MY EX-WIFE AND BEST FRIEND JANET GREENE AND HER ENTIRE FAMILY:
Janet, you, more than anyone, taught me the importance of having a personal relationship with Jesus Christ. Your children, Morgan and Nick, enriched my life as did your entire family. I love you.

TO MY ENTIRE FAMILY, FRIENDS AND COLLEAGUES IN THE LEGAL PROFESSION:
Your presence in my life made my adventure a beautiful ride.

IN MEMORIAM

VIOLET TAYLOR HAWKINS – My fourth grandchild stillborn on August 17, 2021, two weeks before her scheduled delivery. Gone but not forgotten. Rest-in-peace sweet girl.

1
PLAYBOOK

In the beginning, God created the heavens and the earth. Now the earth was formless and empty, darkness was over the surface of the deep, and the Spirit of God was hovering over the waters.
—GENESIS 1:1–2

God created light; God separated Sky and Water; God separated land and seas and provided vegetation; God made the sun, moon, and stars; God filled the waters and sky with fish and birds; God filled the earth with animals. On the Sixth day, God created man and woman. On the seventh day God rested.
—GENESIS 1:3–21; 2:1–3

An Angel of the Lord appeared and advised Joseph that Mary would give birth to a son, to be named Jesus, because he will save His people from their sins.
—MATTHEW 1:20–22

ATHLETE

Every athlete will be subjected to a playbook. Football has one for offense and defense. Basketball has a playbook for winning strategies and plays. Baseball has a playbook designed to maximize a team's strengths and take advantage of an opponent's weaknesses. Even individual sports like golf, tennis, track, and swimming develop playbooks and strategies that enable athletes to perform at their maximum capability. Playbooks are necessary for winning and competing.

GAME OF LIFE

The game of life has one playbook: the Holy Bible. It has two parts: the Old Testament and the New Testament. God's chosen people like Moses, Abraham, Job, David, and King Solomon authored the Old Testament. It preserves the history of God saving His people. It reveals God the Father. It contains numerous prophecies (playbooks) for the coming of a Savior, Jesus Christ. It is God's word.

The New Testament is the second half of God's playbook (the Bible). Followers of Jesus Christ, such as Matthew, Mark, Luke, John, Paul (Saul), and James, wrote it. The New Testament lays out God's plan for the salvation of humankind through Jesus Christ. Jesus fulfilled the prophecies contained in the Old Testament. It provides everyone with a plan for spiritual salvation and eternal life through belief and acceptance of Jesus Christ as Lord and Savior. *Jesus is God in the flesh.*

In the game of life, if you truly want to know God, to have a personal relationship with Jesus Christ, and to receive God's Holy Spirit to guide you on your life's journey, you must make the Bible your playbook. Reading it regularly, praying, and spending time in meditation with the Lord constitute the playbook for playing the game of life.

NOTES, COMMENTS, OR REFLECTIONS

2
BELIEVE

For God so loved the world that He gave His one and only Son, that whoever believes in Him shall not perish but have eternal life.
—JOHN 3:16

For God did not send His Son into the world to condemn the world, but to save the world through Him.
—JOHN 3:17

ATHLETE

Athletes must believe in themselves and their ability to compete. Teammates must believe in each other to achieve success. Coaches must believe in their players and their strategies to win games. Fans like to believe their teams will win every game. Strong beliefs play an important role in winning and competing.

GAME OF LIFE

How many times at a ball game have we seen a fan holding up a banner espousing John 3:16? The message recognizes that fans are, by definition, fanatics. The bearer of such a sign is attempting to reach large audiences with the most important message ever: that God loves the world, that God sacrificed His Son to save sinners, and that whoever believes in Him shall be rewarded with eternal life in heaven. In the game of life, the stakes are high, and no one can afford to lose it. It is a simple message but the most powerful one ever written. Believe!

NOTES, COMMENTS, OR REFLECTIONS

And we know that in all things, God works for the good of those who love Him, who have been called according to His purpose.
—ROMANS 8:28

All authority in Heaven and on earth has been given to Me. Therefore, go and make disciples of all nations, baptizing them in the name of the Father, the Son and the Holy Spirit, teaching them to obey everything I have commanded you. And surely, I am with you always, to the very end of the age.
—MATTHEW 28:18–20

ATHLETE

What is the purpose of athletics? There are several answers to this question, depending on the level at where the athlete is competing. The purpose of Little Leaguers is to have fun. For many, it is a matter of getting and staying physically fit. It improves a young person's mental acuity. It teaches discipline and perseverance. High school sports continue to develop the mind and the body. High school athletes help develop school spirit. High school athletic programs provide talented individuals with the opportunity to attend college on athletic scholarships and earn college degrees.

An athletic program develops leadership skills at all levels. It develops self-esteem. It teaches mutual respect among coaches, players, and opponents. It trains its participants in time management. It supports a life of health and wellness. Those who are outstanding in sports frequently end up playing professional sports or coaching teams, all of which provide a quality standard of life. Athletes, teams, and sports interject energy and vitality in communities.

GAME OF LIFE

In the game of life, one frequently asks, "What is my purpose in life?" In the life of a Christian, the purpose after having accepted Christ as Lord and Savior is to worship, have fellowship, serve, do discipleship, minister and witness to others, and make life better for others. Our purpose in life is to serve Christ, and we do this by serving others—by sharing our blessings and lifting the spirits of others through the gospel of Jesus Christ. What better way to fulfill your life and thereby claim victory in the game of life than by helping others through faith in Christ? Pastor Rick Warren authored an excellent book *The Purpose Driven Life*. There is no greater purpose than serving God. Seek God's purpose for your life.

NOTES, COMMENTS, OR REFLECTIONS

4
VICTORY

*With God we will gain the victory and He
will trample down our enemies.*
—PSALM 60:12

*No one who is born of God will continue to sin,
because God's seed remains in him; he cannot go on
sinning, because he has been born of God.*
—1 JOHN 3:8–9

ATHLETE

Winning has become the measuring stick for athletic success. Win, and you are a hero, a champion. Lose, and you are a failure. *Victory,* however, can come in many forms other than the final score. A famous sportswriter, Grantland Rice, said, "It is not whether you win or lose; it's how you play the game." Gene Autry, a legendary cowboy movie star and owner of the Los Angeles Angels baseball team, was said to have commented, "Well, Grantland Rice can go to [Hades]." In the movie *We Are Marshall,* the head football coach (played by Matthew McConaughey), who succeeded the head coach and team lost in an airplane crash, attempted to rebuild the program. His character, talking to an assistant, said (I'm paraphrasing with my emphasis), "It's not whether we win or lose the game. It's not even how we play the game. *The important thing is that we play the game.*" In life, victory can be achieved even in the face of defeat.

GAME OF LIFE

In the game of life, you were born, and you will die. In between those two events, you will live and play the game of life. *How you play it will determine whether you can claim victory or defeat. With God, you gain eternal victory.* Reject God, and you will lose forever. To achieve victory, how you play the game matters. God laid out a game plan for victory: accept Christ as your Lord and Savior and pursue righteousness. You will experience setbacks and losses in your earthly life, but if you stay in the game, with the Lord's help, you can pull victory from the jaws of defeat. Praise God!

NOTES, COMMENTS, OR REFLECTIONS

5
THE HEAD COACH

*Great is the Lord and most worthy of praise; His
greatness no one can fathom ... The Lord is gracious and
compassionate, slow to anger and rich in love ... The Lord
is good to all; he has compassion on all He has made.*
—PSALM 145:3, 8–9

*Jesus went into the synagogue and began to teach. The people
were amazed at his teaching, because he taught them as
one who had authority, not the teachers of the law.*
—MARK 1:22

ATHLETE

The head coach is the authoritative figure in sports. His objective is to prepare his team to win. He does so by evaluating the opponent's strengths and weaknesses, and determining how to use his team's strengths and disguise his team's weaknesses to take advantage of the opponent and teach his players how to win. Then he lays out a plan, the team practices in preparation for the game, and the team plays the game under the direction of the head coach. In athletics, the head coach is the authoritative figure who makes decisions about players, including who plays and how much. His evaluation determines playing time. Most athletes will tell you that their primary objective is to please the head coach—to obtain his approval. For teams to be successful, there must be mutual respect and trust between players and their coaches.

After Jesus was resurrected from the tomb, He appeared before His disciples and gave them the message in Matthew 28:18–19, namely that all authority rested with Him. *Jesus is the Head Coach in the game of life.* His commission is as true today as it was when He first spoke. In our society, we are constantly looking for heroes, role models, mentors, and individuals with whom we can identify and after whom we can model our lives. Jesus said, "I am the Truth, the Way, the Life" (John 14:6).

Jesus is the one and only Head Coach in the game of life. Acceptance of His authority is putting on the armor to engage in life's battles. His teachings about how to live a righteous life set forth His game plan. Once we accept Him as our Head Coach, we become ministers of His teachings. *We trust and respect Him, which means we fear Him.* Accepting Christ as Lord and Savior relieves His players of all other fears. Jesus coaches us to victory.

NOTES, COMMENTS, OR REFLECTIONS

6
BE FEARLESS

Even though I walk through the valley of the shadow of death, I will fear no evil, for you are with me; your rod and staff comfort me.
—PSALM 23:4

Whatever happens, conduct yourselves in a manner worthy of the Gospel of Christ ... without being frightened in any way by those who oppose you. This is a sign to them that they will be destroyed, but that you will be saved - and that by God.
—PHILIPPIANS 1:27–28

Jesus said, "Do not let your hearts be troubled. Trust in God, trust also in Me."
—JOHN 14:1

ATHLETE

All athletes experience valleys. They can't make a putt, get a base hit, hit a free-throw, or win a game. It is the nature of competition that we experience success and failure. Sometimes the criticism of athletic failures causes the athlete to be depressed, fearful, or afraid of continued failure and criticism. The great athletes who perform under pressure will tell you that the fear of failure never enters their minds. They want to take the last shot, make the winning putt, and score the victorious touchdown—and they have no fear of failing to do so. Hall of Famers play fearlessly.

In the game of life, we fear only God. We achieve victory by placing our hope, trust, and faith in God's word. If God is for us, how can anyone be against us (Rom. 8:31)? There will always be those who want to instill fear in others. They want to dominate, control, and manipulate other lives. Christians know God's goodness and love will follow them all the days of their lives.

Being fearless allows you to take risks in life. You are fearless when you refuse to retreat from a situation despite your fears or insecurities. As Isaiah 12:2 says, "Behold, God is my salvation, I will trust and not be afraid, for the Lord God is my strength, my song, and He has become my salvation." God doesn't want you to live a life of fear or timidity. He wants His followers to trust in Him and be fearless. In the game of life, we achieve victory when we love the Lord and place our hope, trust, and faith in Him.

NOTES, COMMENTS, OR REFLECTIONS

7
STRENGTH

I can do everything through God who gives me strength.
—**Philippians 4:13**

I love you, O Lord, my strength.
It is God who arms me with strength and makes my way perfect.
—**Psalm 18:1, 32**

ATHLETE

Many adjectives are used to describe an athlete—speed, hand-eye coordination, and jumping ability, to name a few. But perhaps none are more important than strength. Weight rooms are prevalent at every level of sports, beginning in junior high school and extending into professional sports. Strength gives one the ability to persevere, sustain punishment to the body, and provide punishment to opponents in contact sports. Professional athletes and college athletes are frequently evaluated based on their strength. Strength training in sports is a year-round requirement to improve and reach your maximum ability. Staying in good physical condition will not only help you in sports but also help provide a better quality of life outside of sports.

GAME OF LIFE

In the game of life, Christians draw their physical, emotional, and mental strength from the Lord. *When we trust in God, we will not be afraid.* When our faith is strong, we will continue to persevere in the face of adversity.

God will provide you with the strength to accomplish your goals and show you the path to follow to maximize your ability. When you are strong, you can deal with your problems and help others with theirs. When you have strength, God will get you through the criticism you will face. *Strength God gives and faith and trust in God's plan for your life will give you confidence that surpasses any life performance.* "The Lord gives strength to the weary, increases the power of the weak, and those whose hope is in the Lord will renew their strength, and they will soar on wings like eagles" (Isaiah 4:28–29, 31). *Victory goes to the strong believers in the game of life.*

NOTES, COMMENTS, OR REFLECTIONS

8
PLAYING BY THE RULES

If anyone competes as an athlete, he does not receive the victor's crown unless he competes according to the rules.
—2 Timothy 2:5

Whoever can be trusted with very little can also be trusted with much, and whoever is dishonest with very little will also be dishonest with much.
—Luke 16:10–11

ATHLETE

Playing by the rules is important in every athletic event. "Cheaters never win, and winners never cheat" is an applicable saying in all sports competitions. Rules of the game are there to protect the integrity of the game and the participants. Athletes need to read, understand, and comply with the rules governing their sport. Dishonesty in sports brings shame. Using performance-enhancing drugs is cheating. Faking injuries is cheating. Fighting, cursing, name-calling, giving low blows, and shaving points are all examples of unwarranted and inappropriate actions by athletes.

GAME OF LIFE

The Bible sets forth God's rules for playing the game of life. In Exodus 20:3–17, God gives us His Ten Commandments.

1. You shall have no other gods before me.
2. You shall have no idols.
3. You shall not misuse the Lord's name.
4. You shall remember the Sabbath.
5. Honor your mother and father.
6. You shall not kill.
7. You shall not commit adultery.
8. You shall not steal.
9. You shall not give false testimony.
10. You shall not covet.

These are the rules for living your life. During life, everyone will violate one or more of these rules. God recognizes that, knowing that no human is perfect. So, God made a perfect human being in Jesus Christ, who came to earth to atone for the sins of men and women. *Accept Christ as Lord and Savior, and your sins are forgiven—forever.*

God also gave us two of His greatest rules to follow (Luke 10:27):

1. Love God with all your heart, strength, mind, and soul.
2. Love your neighbors as you love yourself.

God doesn't want us to hate our enemies. His rules don't allow hatred for other people. Hatred is reserved for evil. God wants us to love and pray for our enemies (Matthew 5:44). Leave the punishment of rule breakers to God. When you play by God's rules in the game of life, you win.

NOTES, COMMENTS, OR REFLECTIONS

9
PREPARATION

No eye has seen, no ear has heard, no mind has conceived
what God has prepared for those who love him.
—1 CORINTHIANS 2:9

Preach the Word; be prepared in season and out of season: correct,
rebuke and encourage—with great patience and careful instruction.
—2 TIMOTHY 4:2

Prepare the way for the Lord, make straight paths for Him.
—MATTHEW 3:3

ATHLETE

Many coaches in different sports have said the "will to win" is easy since everyone has a will to win, but more important is the "will to prepare to win." These coaches recognized that winning is a by-product of preparation. Athletes need to prepare year-round to participate in their sport by staying physically fit, being mentally and emotionally fit and prepared, and working to improve the skills necessary to effectively play the games. Many underdogs win games against more talented athletic teams by outworking themselves and being better prepared.

GAME OF LIFE

In the game of life, it's important to stay physically and emotionally fit. It is more important to stay spiritually fit. How does one become spiritually fit? This is done through prayer, Bible reading, meditation time with the

Lord, and associating with like-minded Christians. It means resisting the temptations constantly thrown at us, namely, drugs, sex, alcohol, cheating, greed, and pride. Jesus warns us in Matthew 26:41 to "watch and pray so that you will not fall into temptation, for the spirit is willing, but the body is weak."

Spiritual preparation needs to be ingrained in your daily life. Ask God to be with you daily, to direct you away from sin, to lead you on a path of righteousness and purpose, and to help you resist worldly temptations. The more time you spend with God, the better prepared you will be to claim victory in the game of life.

NOTES, COMMENTS, OR REFLECTIONS

10
ADVERSITY

If God is for us, who can be against us?
—ROMANS 8:31

*Then they cried out to the Lord in their trouble,
and he brought them out of their distress.*
—PSALM 107:28

*For the Lord gives wisdom and from His mouth
comes knowledge and understanding.*
—PROVERBS 2:6

ATHLETE

All athletes experience adversity. Physical injury adversely affects an athlete's ability to compete. Mental and emotional adversity impacts the athlete's ability to focus. It comes in the form of competition—competition against another team or a player attempting to take his or her position. Good, however, can come from adversity. Athletes learn from their failures. They become better prepared because of their losses. When you confront adversity, you will learn more about your strengths and weaknesses than you do about your success.

GAME OF LIFE

In situations of adversity, conflict, trouble, and problems, God is there for you—but you must seek Him. God has a plan for your life. It may not be your plan. It may not be what you want. It will be what God sees as your need. It will be consistent with God's plan for your life, for your purpose in life. God's plan is to prosper you. Following God's plan for your life and keeping His commandments in your heart "will prolong your life many years, and bring you prosperity" (Proverbs 3:1–2). "Preserve sound judgment and discernment, do not let them out of your sight, they will be life for you" (Proverbs 3: 1, 21). In the game of life, your faith in God and *acceptance of Christ as Savior* will arm you to win victory over adversity.

NOTES, COMMENTS, OR REFLECTIONS

11
REFEREES

Do not judge, and you will not be judged. Do not condemn,
and you will not be condemned. Forgive, and you will
be forgiven. Give, and it will be given to you.
—Luke 6:37–38

If any one of you is without sin, let him
be the first to throw a stone.
—John 8:7

ATHLETE

One of the most difficult jobs in all sports is refereeing sports competitions. The referee is there to make everyone play by the rules, to call rule violations as he or she sees them, and to make decisions without bias or prejudice. Referees are human; they will make mistakes. The athlete shouldn't judge or condemn the referee's decision. It is permissible to ask for clarification of a call, but this should be done in a professional manner.

Athletes cannot allow bad refereeing to get into their heads. It will impact the players' performance. Athletes' negative reactions can result in a technical foul or penalty to be enforced. An athlete can be disqualified for having too many technical fouls, for cursing or subjecting a referee to abuse, or for making physical contact with a referee. Athletes need to play ball, leave the refereeing to the referees, and let the coaches question the referees' calls.

In the game of life, God is our referee. He has laid out the rules for us to play by as we journey through life. It is for Him to judge our compliance with the rules. It is for Him to determine the penalty for our violations of His rules. God will listen to our explanations of rule violations, but His decisions will be made based on what He sees in a person's heart. Our actions speak much louder than our words. He has given us much. How have we used His blessings? He has forgiven our sins through the sacrifice of Jesus Christ. Have we accepted Christ as Savior? Have we forgiven our trespassers? Are we critical or judgmental of others' conduct? Are we judging others? *God wants us to be givers, not takers.* He doesn't want us to judge the conduct of others, especially their relationship with the Lord. He will make those judgments. He wants us to love, honor, and obey His rules in the game of life. By doing so, we achieve victory.

NOTES, COMMENTS, OR REFLECTIONS

12
COURAGE

Be on your guard, stand firm in the faith; be men/women
of courage; be strong and do everything in Love.
—1 CORINTHIANS 16:13–14

My Father, if it possible, may this cup be taken
from me. Yet, not as I will, but as You will.
—MATTHEW 26:39

So do not fear, for I am with you; do not be dismayed,
for I am your God. I will strengthen you and help you;
I will uphold you with my righteous right hand.
—ISAIAH 41:10

ATHLETE

Being an athlete takes courage. In many sports, you will fail many times more than you succeed. A baseball player whose batting average is an excellent .300 fails 70 percent of the time. Lose to a rival, and your team will be vilified. Drop a winning touchdown pass in football, and you will be described as a failure. Finish second, and you will be considered the "first loser."

Fans will be critical, sometimes even in victory. The media can be unrelenting in its criticism of athletes and teams. Social media will paint you as a loser. It takes courage for athletes to endure the criticism that comes with sports participation. What young athletes must remember is that they will be measured not by how many times they are knocked down but by how many times they get up. How did they perform in the face of adversity? All anyone can ask of athletes is that they give their very best.

GAME OF LIFE

In the game of life, God tells us to stand firm, keep the faith, and act out of love. God is our refuge. He will give you courage and strength as you journey through life. He has already given sinners victory over evil and death through Jesus Christ. It isn't a coincidence that many people find Christ during a time of failure. When they have been defeated, divorced, knocked down by addictions, declared bankruptcy, and imprisoned, they will find their courage to keep going in God Almighty.

When we are suffering from depression, gloom, or hopelessness, He will be our refuge. He will provide us with the courage we need to continue our journey. He will provide us with victory by giving us the courage to face whatever life throws at us.

NOTES, COMMENTS, OR REFLECTIONS

13
THE NUMBER THIRTEEN

But I trust in your unfailing love: my heart rejoices in your salvation. I will sing to the Lord, for He has been good to me.
—PSALM 13:5–6

He who scorns instruction will pay for it; but he who respects a command is rewarded.
—PROVERBS 13:13

You call me 'Teacher' and 'Lord' and rightly so, for that is what I am.
—JOHN 13:13

ATHLETE

Every athlete has his or her favorite number. Professional athletes have been known to pay thousands of dollars to another teammate to wear a certain number. The greatest running back of all time, Jim Brown, wore number thirty-two, triggering a demand for that number by running backs in the NFL. Michael Jordan wore number twenty-three, which resulted in numerous basketball players requesting to wear that number. Peyton Manning, the Super Bowl-winning quarterback, wore the number eighteen to honor his father and brother.

In many instances, high schools, colleges, and professional sports teams retire the number of an athlete whose contributions to the team and sport have been unsurpassed. There is one number many athletes shun, the number thirteen. The number stirs the emotions of superstitious fans. It is considered the unluckiest number in sports. Some professional sports teams have banned the wearing of number thirteen. Some argue that this number represents death.

GAME OF LIFE

Some biblical scholars have suggested that the number thirteen represents Satan, evil, wickedness, devils, and everything vile connected to them. Some point out that Jesus's betrayal was by Judas, who occupied the thirteenth seat at the Last Supper. Other scholars believe it is the symbol of rebellion.

At the end of the day, thirteen is just a number. Man's interpretation of the number as being unlucky is based on superstition. Superstition is based on a lack of one's faith. The Bible doesn't support superstitious beliefs and considers them idolatry. God teaches us that nothing is done outside His control. To many Christians, the number thirteen is magical, in that it contains two very important biblical numbers: one and three. *We have one God in the form of three entities: God the Father, God the Son, and God the Holy Spirit.* This is the Holy Trinity. In the game of life, Christians don't believe in superstitions but rather believe that God is our teacher, our Lord. It is in His trusting love that we place our faith.

NOTES, COMMENTS, OR REFLECTIONS

14
ANGER

*Everyone should be quick to listen, slow to
speak, and slow to become angry.*
—JAMES 1:19

*In your anger, do not sin. Do not let the son go down while
you are still angry, and do not give the devil a foothold.*
—EPHESIANS 4:26–27

ATHLETE

Anger among athletes is inevitable. Competition breeds passion. Passion under certain circumstances breeds anger and resentment. Uncontrolled anger leads to pushing, shoving, fouling, fighting, cursing, disqualifying, being suspended, and potentially losing. Controlled anger, on the other hand, can serve as a motivating force. Used properly, anger can enhance an athlete's competitive juices and encourage his or her desire to defeat the opponent. Controlled anger can propel an athlete or team to victory. Athletes can control anger by becoming slow to anger, by thinking about the consequences before acting or reacting, and by focusing on the goals to be accomplished.

GAME OF LIFE

The game of life presents many opportunities for participants to be angry. No one likes to lose. No one wants to fail. When we follow God's direction to be "slow to anger" and act out of love and forgiveness, we can turn anger into controlled anger. We must be compassionate and gracious. Psalm

103:8 says we shouldn't sin in our anger. God tells His followers to "turn the other cheek" rather than physically confront the adversary. In Matthew 5:39, God tells us not to seek revenge but rather to leave revenge to Him. In the game of life, you win when you control your anger. *You will learn more in life from your losses and failures than from your wins and successes. This is called "experience."*

NOTES, COMMENTS, OR REFLECTIONS

15
COMMITMENT

All a man's ways seem innocent to him, but motives are weighed by the Lord. Commit to the Lord whatever you do, and your plans will succeed.
—**PROVERBS 16:2–3**

Now I commit you to God and to the word of His grace, which can build you up and give you an inheritance among all those who are sanctified.
—**ACTS 20:32**

ATHLETE

At the very beginning of your athletic career, you will repeatedly hear the term *commitment*. Coaches preach commitment—commit to the team, to preparation, to the game plan, to physical fitness, to serving, and to winning. In sports, the concept of commitment is a core value. You cannot achieve individual or team success without commitment. Commitment means dedicating yourself, your efforts, to reaching or achieving your goals. When an athlete is committed to a cause or activity, he or she foregoes freedom of action and focuses on doing whatever is necessary to achieve the goals and objective of the team. Most coaches will choose a committed athlete over one who is more talented but less committed.

GAME OF LIFE

Commitment plays a huge role in the game of life. Commitment to marriage, a job, raising children, friends, organizations, and church plays an important role in determining the quality of one's life. *The single most important commitment anyone on earth will ever make is accepting Jesus Christ as Lord and Savior.* Once we commit to accepting Him as Savior, we act on that commitment by serving Him, glorifying Him, and offering Him praise and thanksgiving for the blessings He bestows. We commit to sinning less, walking in His path of righteousness, and doing good in the world. This commitment leads to victory in the game of life.

NOTES, COMMENTS, OR REFLECTIONS

The greatest among you will be your servant. For whoever exalts himself will be humbled, and whoever humbles himself will be exalted.
—MATTHEW 23:11–12

Let them praise the name of the Lord, for His name alone is exalted, his splendor is above the earth and the heavens.
—PSALM 148:13

Yours, O Lord, is the greatness and the power and the glory and the majesty and the splendor, for everything in Heaven and Earth is yours.
—1 CHRONICLES 29:11

ATHLETE

In athletics, the term *goat* has a dual meaning, and both meanings are in direct opposition to each other. When it is spelled G-O-A-T, the sports reference means the "greatest of all time." Tom Brady, winner of seven Super Bowls, has been called the GOAT in professional football. Michael Jordan received the same acclaim in basketball. Tiger Woods is arguably the GOAT in professional golf. These are all athletes who not only excelled at the highest level in their respective sports but also won many championships. Greatness is defined by successful accomplishment.

The other sports reference using the term *goat* is defined as a player who makes a critical mistake or an error that cost his or her team the game and/or championship. The most memorable usage of *goat* in this context describes Bill Buckner, the first basemen for the Boston Red Sox, who allowed a routine ground ball to go through his legs, letting the winning run score and costing his team the game and ultimately the World Series.

GAME OF LIFE

Greatness in the game of life comes from serving God and others. Service to others keeps us focused on their needs, not on ourselves. Greatness means sacrificing yourself for the benefit of others. God is clearly our GOAT. He is the one and only GOAT. He proved it when, because of His love for all mankind, He sacrificed His Son, Jesus Christ, to pay for the sins of all mankind forever. Think about that.

No parents would offer their child as a sacrifice to pay for the sins of all mankind forever, because of the overwhelming love parents have for their children and the innate quality of wanting to protect them from harm. Yet God so loved the world that He gave His only begotten Son so that whoever believes and accepts Him shall not perish but shall have life in heaven forever. *What an awesome God we have!* Jesus paid for our sins, a debt He didn't owe. Our sin is our debt, but we have no way of paying for our sin except through the belief and acceptance of Jesus Christ as Savior. *Don't be a goat; instead, accept Christ and live eternity with the GOAT. Claim victory in the game of life.*

NOTES, COMMENTS, OR REFLECTIONS

17
LIFE IS A MARATHON

Be temperate, worthy of respect, self-controlled, and sound in faith, in love and in endurance.
—TITUS 2:1

Surely goodness and love will follow me all the days of my life, and I will dwell in the house of the Lord forever.
—PSALM 23:6

Now we know that if the earthly tent we live in is destroyed, we have a building from God, an eternal house in Heaven, not built by human hands.
—2 CORINTHIANS 5:1

ATHLETE

Marathon runners are unique athletes. They train by running thousands of miles annually. They possess qualities that will benefit all athletes: focus, motivation, resiliency, preparation, inspiration, and a high pain threshold. Their race is more than twenty-six miles, during which they will experience pain, suffering, exhaustion, and dehydration. At the end of the race, they will be physically, mentally, and emotionally spent. If you finish the race, you are considered a winner, no matter in which position you finish. Your reward is the confidence you gain from facing a daunting challenge you successfully met.

GAME OF LIFE

Life is not a sprint. It is a marathon. In the game of life, you will be on a journey that requires many of the same characteristics that benefit a marathon runner. You will have highs and lows. You will have successes and failures. You will have joy and sadness. You may experience financial setbacks or win the lottery. God has equipped you to run the race. His love, grace, and mercy through Jesus Christ are there for your acceptance. They will bring you peace and calmness in all situations. God will never let you suffer more than you can bear. Just believe, accept Christ as Savior, and run the race of life. At the end, you will receive your reward: life eternal in heaven. It won't make any difference where you finished in the race, just that you finished. *Victory is yours through Christ.*

NOTES, COMMENTS, OR REFLECTIONS

18

GET IN THE GAME

Come, follow me and I will make you fishers of men.
—MATTHEW 4:19

*If anyone would come after Me, he must deny himself and take up
his cross and follow Me. For whoever wants to save his life will lose
it, but whoever loses his life for Me will find it. What good will it
be for a man if he gains the whole world yet forfeits his soul.*
—MATTHEW 16:24–26

*Therefore, if anyone is in Christ, he is a new creation;
the old has gone, the new has come. All this is from God,
who reconciled us to Himself through Christ.*
—2 CORINTHIANS 5:17–18

ATHLETE

"Get in the game" can mean different things to an athlete. Those words
from a coach to a player may mean the athlete should enter the game as a
substitute for another player, who has been in the game and needs to rest or
is failing to perform. If it is said to a player already in the game, it can mean
for him or her to focus, to get one's head in the game. The goal or objective
of every athlete is to get in the game, participate, play, and perform well.
Athletes in team sports recognize that the coach determines who plays and
how much. Consequently, athletes like to please their coaches. They do
so through preparing, understanding the game plan, and demonstrating
performance in practice and games. You cannot impact the game if you
aren't in it.

In the game of life, we have a choice. We can refuse to play, or we can get in the game and have an impact on not only our lives but also on the lives of others. Jesus has challenged us to follow Him. There are consequences either way.

If you fail to accept His challenge and choose not to get in the game, then the consequences are catastrophic. If, however, you accept Christ's challenge to get in the game, He expects your actions to be consistent with your professed faith. He wants you to share the good news about the game you have chosen to play. He wants you to walk by faith, run with assurance, and win the game He has offered you. He wants you to share your win with others. He will provide you with all the equipment you need once you get in the game.

NOTES, COMMENTS, OR REFLECTIONS

19
RESPECT YOUR OPPONENT

So, in everything, do to others what you would have them do to you.
—**MATTHEW 7:12**

God opposes the proud but gives grace to the humble. Submit yourself to God. Resist the Devil. Come near to God and He will come near to you.
—**JAMES 3:6–8**

Whoever turns a sinner from the error of his way will save him from death and cover a multitude of sins.
—**JAMES 5:20**

ATHLETE

Rivalries are a staple of sports competitions. In college, rivalries exist between athletic teams located in the same conference, state, or adjoining states. In pro sports, rivalries exist between teams with rich heritage and traditions, and between teams that regularly compete for championships. Rivalries generate fan support, bragging rights, and traditions. Many observers suggest that rival teams hate each other or that their fans and players hate each other.

There should be mutual respect between rival teams and their fans. Opponents should be respected. Cheating, intentionally trying to injure your opponent, yelling, screaming, and cursing your opponent are all acts that show disrespect not only for your opponent but also for the game. When the game is over and your opponent has won, just congratulate him or her and know there will be another day when the game will turn in your favor.

GAME OF LIFE

In the game of life, God teaches us to respect—indeed love—those who oppose us. He gave us the Golden Rule to live by. Do to others as you would have them do to you. Society is filled with too much hate for people whose thoughts and ideas are different from one another. God doesn't support hatred among people. Hate is reserved for acts of evil. Respect your opponent.

Respect those who don't believe in God or are antagonistic toward Him. Show them the error of their way by following the Lord's teachings of love, grace, and mercy. Help draw such people to Christ by allowing them to see His presence in you through your faith, love, kindness, and righteous treatment of others. When you do, you can turn sinners, atheists, and agnostics into Christians, who are supportive of the game of life in Jesus Christ. *In any event, pray for those who refuse Christ.*

NOTES, COMMENTS, OR REFLECTIONS

20
CARRY THE BALL

For I was hungry, and you gave me something to eat.
I was thirsty and you gave me something to drink. I
was a stranger and you invited me in. I needed clothes
and you clothed me. I was sick and you looked after
me. I was in prison and you came to visit me.
—MATTHEW 25:35–36

God chose you to be saved through the sanctifying
work of the Spirit and through belief in the truth.
He called you to this through our gospel, that you
might have the glory of our Lord Jesus Christ.
—2 THESSALONIANS 2:13–14

ATHLETE

"Carry the ball" is a sports metaphor reflecting the responsibility for its safekeeping. It is the exact opposite of "dropping the ball," which suggests failure to protect the ball. The team's goals are to advance the ball toward the goal and complete the goal of scoring. Carrying the ball is a way to tell the ball carrier, "You have a responsibility to the team to 'carry the ball' toward the goal." The coach may penalize players who drop the ball and take them out of the game. If you are successful in carrying the ball, then you are responsible and trustworthy. This metaphor is all about athletes taking responsibility for their actions and accountability for their performance.

Christians have a responsibility, for which they will be held accountable. In the game of life, God wants His followers to share the good news of Jesus Christ. The apostle Paul (Saul) is the perfect example of a Christian who, after accepting Christ as Savior, turned from his sinful ways and carried the ball. In other words, he shared the gospel of Jesus Christ throughout the land. Paul's preaching, teaching and witnessing as chronicled in the New Testament gave birth to the Christian religion. Paul never strayed from his message that Jesus Christ was God in the flesh, that He died and was resurrected by the Lord in payment for the sins of all mankind and for the eternal salvation of anyone who accepts Christ as Savior.

From those humble beginnings, the Christian religion has grown to be the largest religion in the world, having more than 2.5 billion followers of Jesus Christ. In the game of life, Christians share the good news of the gospel—that Christ has risen, that sins are forgiven for those who believe and follow, and that Christians should carry the ball by sharing it with others.

NOTES, COMMENTS, OR REFLECTIONS

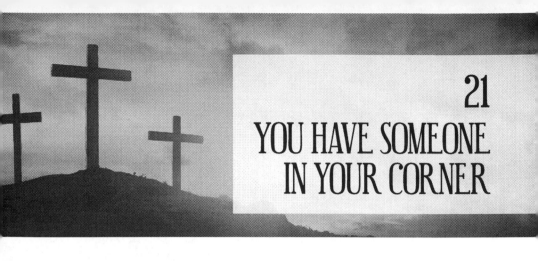

21
YOU HAVE SOMEONE IN YOUR CORNER

For where two or three come together in My Name, there I am with you.
—MATTHEW 18:20

For this reason, ever since I heard about your faith in the Lord Jesus and your love for all the saints, I have not stopped giving thanks for you, remembering you in my prayers. I keep asking that the God of our Lord Jesus Christ, the glorious Father, may give you the Spirit of wisdom and revelation, so that you may know Him better. I pray also that the eyes of your heart may be enlightened in order that you may know the hope to which He has called you; the riches of His glorious inheritance in the saints and his incomparably great power for us who believe.
—EPHESIANS 1:15–19

ATHLETE

Boxers need to have someone in their corner. Usually, it is their manager. Athletes need a lot of people to be in their corner: coaches, parents, teammates, trainers, medical personnel, and support groups. The unconditional support that comes from those in your corner is paramount to success in the sports arena. In sports, you will experience the "thrill of victory" and the "agony of defeat." The people in your corner will be there for you whether you win or lose. These same people will help keep you grounded when things are going great and will pick you up when things aren't going so well. Athletes who can identify those individuals who are in their corner will benefit greatly from their support.

GAME OF LIFE

In the game of life, we need a support group. We all need someone in our corner. Life throws a lot of things at you, both good and bad. The key to handling these ups and downs is to stabilize your emotions. Don't get too high when things are going well, nor too low when things are going bad. Having someone in your corner brings balance to your life. Choose good people for friends. Associate with people who are honest and trustworthy. Find friends and supporters who share Christian values. *You not only need to find someone to have in your corner but also need to be that someone in somebody else's corner.*

Like the apostle Paul, Christians are called on to use their wisdom, judgment, and faith in providing support to those who need someone in their corner. Christians know they will always have someone in their corner—Jesus Christ. His message of love, grace, mercy, righteousness, kindness, goodness, and forgiveness will resonate with anyone who chooses to believe. *Having Jesus Christ in your corner will bring victory in the game of life.*

NOTES, COMMENTS, OR REFLECTIONS

22
MONEYBALL

You cannot serve both God and money.
—MATTHEW 6:24

People who want to get rich fall into temptation and a trap into many foolish and harmful desires that plunge them into ruin and destruction. For the love of money is the root of all kinds of evil. Some people, eager for money, have wandered from the faith and pierced themselves with many griefs.
—1 TIMOTHY 6:7–10

ATHLETE

Moneyball is one of the best sports movies ever made. The movie's basic premise is that the collective wisdom of baseball insiders (players, managers, coaches, and scouts) on how to build a championship team is flawed. Most professional baseball organizations pursued a philosophy of throwing large sums of money and long-term contracts at star baseball players as the route to a World Series. In *Moneyball*, the general manager of the Oakland Athletics believed success could be found through sports analytics. They pursued undervalued players, whom statistical analysis showed performed the right task at the right time. The team experienced significant success.

In the past several years, sports analytics have become a significant part of college and pro sports. Throwing large sums of money at players is still followed by a lot of organizations, but more attention is given to a player's statistical performance. Sports analytics have also become part of playing decisions (e.g., whether to go for it on the fourth down versus punting or kicking a field goal in football, which free throw shooters need to be at the end of a close basketball game, or who should pinch hit in a baseball game where a hit is needed in a close game). The pursuit of money isn't always the best way to build a team.

GAME OF LIFE

In the game of life, knowing Jesus Christ as Lord and Savior makes one as rich as anyone can be. Accumulating wealth becomes sinful and destructive when money becomes your God. You cannot serve both money and God. Jesus said that a rich man has about as much chance of getting into heaven as a camel passing through the eye of a needle (Matthew 20:24). Being wealthy or accumulating wealth isn't sinful.

The Lord looks at how you accumulate wealth and what you do with your wealth. There are wealthy pastors, athletes, entertainers, and business entrepreneurs who have accepted Christ as Savior and use their wealth as a blessing to make life better for others. God will look at what you do with the blessings He bestows on you to determine whether money is your God. So gather all the riches you can but share them with those in need. Never make money your God. Having confidence in your salvation through Jesus Christ is as rich as anyone could hope to be. *Christ's love makes you rich.*

NOTES, COMMENTS, OR REFLECTIONS

SHARE THE BALL

*Do not withhold good from those who deserve
it, when it's in your power to act.*
—PROVERBS 3:27

*Command those who are rich in this present world not to be arrogant nor
to put their hope in wealth, which is so uncertain, but to put their hope in
God who richly provides us with everything for our enjoyment. Command
them to do good, to be rich in good deeds, and to be willing to share.*
—1 TIMOTHY 6:17–18

The righteous give generously.
—PSALM 37:21

ATHLETE

"Share the ball" is a basketball idiom coaches use to get players to be
unselfish, to get everyone involved in the game, and to see that players are
rewarded for their efforts. The concept promotes teamwork. Teamwork
promotes success. Team success promotes winning. Winning brings
glory and praise to the entire team. Sharing the ball is a fundamental
requirement for success in team sports. Sharing the ball makes a team hard
to defend. Sharing the ball will get the best opportunity to score.

GAME OF LIFE

God favors those who are willing to give, to share the ball. Christians
should be givers. One of the primary purposes for which God placed us

here is to make life better for others by sharing the ball. God will provide you with more than you need, so share His blessings with those who deserve it and are in need. Gifts, large and small, can change people's lives. The sharing of a blessing will bring the giver a victory in the game of life. Give to the church, the poor, and the charities that seek to make life better for the less fortunate.

A Harvard business professor, a devout Christian, was asked what God would say to him at the "pearly gates." His response was that God's first statement to him would be, "Tell me what you did to make life better for others with the blessings I bestowed upon you." As you journey through life, ask yourself how you are preparing yourself to answer God's question: *How did you share the ball?*

NOTES, COMMENTS, OR REFLECTIONS

And the angel said, "Joseph, son of David, do not be afraid to take Mary home as your wife, because what is conceived in her is from the Holy Spirit. She will give birth to a son, and you are to give Him the name Jesus because He will save His people from their sins.
—MATTHEW 1:20–21

The angel said to the women: "Do not be afraid, for I know that you are looking for Jesus, who was crucified. He is not here; He has risen, just as He said. Come and see the place where He lay. Then go quickly and tell His disciples, "He has risen from the dead and is going ahead of you into Galilee. There you will see him."
—MATTHEW 28:5–7

ATHLETE

Sports competitions are full of so-called miracles. In the sports world, the miracle of miracles was when the American hockey team, composed of college amateurs, defeated the Russian hockey team, composed of professional veterans, in the gold medal game in the 1980 Olympics. In pro football, there is the "Minnesota miracle" in 2018, when the Vikings scored on a sixty-one-yard touchdown pass on the last play of the game to defeat the New Orleans Saints in the NFL playoffs. In college, there is the "Bluegrass miracle" in a 2002 football game between LSU and Kentucky. On the last play of the game, LSU scored on a seventy-four-yard touchdown pass to defeat the Kentucky Wildcats 33 to 30.

In baseball, Don Larson, a New York Yankee pitcher, pitched the only perfect game against the Brooklyn Dodgers to win the 1956 World Series.

And who can forget the miracle football game in 2022 between the Buffalo Bills and the Kansas City Chiefs? The two teams combined to score twenty-five points in the last two minutes of the game, with the Chiefs ultimately winning. Every sport has some last-minute miracle that allowed a team or an individual to "pull victory from the jaws of defeat" on a last-minute winning play. "Miracles" in sports are rare but do occur.

GAME OF LIFE

The two greatest miracles in the history of the world are chronicled in the Bible, in Mathew 1:20–21 (the virgin birth of Jesus) and Matthew 26:5–7 (the resurrection of Jesus Christ following His crucifixion). God performed these miracles to save people from their sins. God came to earth as Jesus Christ. He walked among people, teaching and preaching what has become known as the gospel. He performed miracles by healing the blind, the sick, and those with leprosy. He raised people from death. He restored eyesight to the blind; He fed thousands with a basket containing a few loaves of bread and a small number of fish. He exorcized demons from a young girl.

Jesus performed many miracles. He provided standards by which to live. He pronounced commandments that, if followed, would make the world a better place. He claimed to be the Messiah, who was prophesied in the Old Testament as being the Savior. He told the truth. He was crucified for it. God wasn't through performing miracles. He raised Jesus from the dead. After His resurrection, which His disciples and many others witnessed, He was brought home to heaven, where He sits on the right hand of God, the Father Almighty.

Why did God do this? The answer is found in John 3:16. He loved the world so much that He wanted to provide imperfect people with an opportunity to be reconciled with Him, a perfect God, and reside with Him in heaven for eternity. "For all have sinned and come short of the glory of God" (Romans 3:23). In the game of life, there is one last miracle for those willing to accept Jesus Christ as Lord and Savior. By accepting

Jesus Christ as Lord and Savior, all your sins (past, present, and future) will be forgiven, and you will dwell in the house of the Lord forever. Just win, baby, the game of life.

NOTES, COMMENTS, OR REFLECTIONS

25
GO THE DISTANCE

But keep your Head in all situations, endure hardship.
—2 TIMOTHY 4:5

He who stands firm to the end will be saved.
—MARK 13:13

Perseverance must finish its work so that you may be mature and complete, not lacking anything.
—JAMES 1:4

ATHLETE

In sports, one "goes the distance" when he or she carries through a course of action to completion. Physical and mental endurance is required to go the distance. The athlete must work through exhaustion, pain, and hardship—all factors that can cause an athlete to quit, give up, or give in. Those who go the distance and finish the race experience mental and physical euphoria. Going the distance requires training, preparation, and mental toughness. Many sporting events have overtimes, extra innings, and sudden-death playoffs. These require athletes to be physically fit and mentally strong. They require commitment. Even if you fail to win, the task of completing the race gives a strong sense of self-gratification.

GAME OF LIFE

In the game of life, God calls His people to endure hardship, stay the course, and stand firm with Him. In doing so, many nonbelievers will criticize them, but they go the distance with their faith.

By strengthening your faith and placing your hope and trust in Jesus Christ, you will endure and stand firm to the end. Endurance is a key indicator of spiritual fitness. The pain and suffering Christ endured on the cross was for God's people, sinners, and all mankind to the very end of the earth. *Christ went the distance for you.* He suffered mockery and humiliation, but He never lost focus on His mission. He endured to the end, saying, "Father forgive them, for they do not know what they are doing" (Luke 23:34). *Stand firm in your faith by going the distance and enduring hardships.*

NOTES, COMMENTS, OR REFLECTIONS

26
MONDAY-MORNING QUARTERBACK

Forget the former things, do not dwell on the past.
—ISAIAH 43:18

Therefore, if anyone is in Christ, he is a new creation, the old has gone, the new has come.
—2 CORINTHIANS 5:16

For I know the plans I have for you, declares the Lord, plans to prosper you, and not to harm you, plans to give you hope and a future.
—JEREMIAH 29:11

ATHLETE

The Monday-morning quarterback holds the greatest position in sports. It is played by individuals who observed but didn't play the game about which they are "quarterbacking." They possess a unique skill: twenty-twenty hindsight. They can tell you exactly what someone should have done but didn't. They can tell you who lost the game and how it was lost. They don't have to pass or run the ball. They don't stand in the pocket and face three-hundred-pound linemen trying to tackle them. They are never injured in battle. Rather, they sit in the comfort of their dwelling, and after the game is over, they tell you the exact play that should have been run to change the outcome.

They are "fans," which is short for "fanatics." Many are sportswriters, most of whom never played the game. They look at the past and criticize the athlete who participated in the game. In their minds, they are never wrong, and the outcome would have been different had they been in charge. Many college athletes can tune out the Monday-morning quarterback. Many who play the game never read about it afterward because they know what is done is over with, and the objective is to learn from one's mistakes and prepare for the next game. Athletes should ignore the Monday-morning quarterback.

GAME OF LIFE

In the game of life, God tells us the past doesn't define us and therefore shouldn't be dwelled on. God wants us to learn from our mistakes, seek repentance for our sins, and focus on the future. God has a plan for every life that seeks His will. Those plans will prosper one's future. God's plans will give you hope and direction. Lives have been ruined by those who dwell on the past, regret decisions made, and wish for an opportunity to change the past. In the game of life, we live for today and tomorrow. We seek God's will for our lives. God will equip us to handle life going forward if we seek His guidance. Jesus died on the cross for the forgiveness of our sins. There is no need for Monday-morning quarterbacking in the game of life because God has forgiven those who accept Christ as Savior. Carry Christ with you daily and let Him be your quarterback.

NOTES, COMMENTS, OR REFLECTIONS

27
ACCEPTANCE

Listen to advice an accept instruction,
and in the end you will be wise.
—**PROVERBS 19:20**

Accept one another, just as Christ accepted
you, in order to bring praise to God.
—**ROMANS 15:7**

I tell you the truth, whoever accepts anyone I send accepts
me; and whoever accepts me accepts the one who sent me.
—**JOHN 13:20**

ATHLETE

The concept of acceptance is pervasive throughout sports. Athletes want their teammates and coaches to accept them. The coach wants players to accept teaching, coaching, and game planning. Teams love to accept awards for accomplishments. Professional athletes want the franchise to accept their salary demands. Franchise owners want fans to accept the team and purchase tickets. Referees want the coaches and players to accept their rulings. Sports media want players to accept their questions and criticism. Game winners want fans to accept their efforts. Winners want to accept winning with grace and dignity. A player, coach, or team can be defined by how they accept winning and losing.

Acceptance plays a huge role in the game of life. As we journey through life, we will be confronted daily with situations we must either accept or reject. Frequently, the choice will be between accepting God's way or the ways of the world. God wants you to accept His way. It begins by accepting Jesus Christ as Lord and Savior. God wants you to accept His grace and mercy. God wants you to accept His forgiveness. God wants you to accept a life of goodness and righteousness filled with love, patience, passion, sharing, and prosperity. You will see many Christians wearing wristbands with the initials WWJD (What Would Jesus Do?). When confronted with choices between worldly acceptance and God's acceptance, choose what Jesus would do. He will never fail you.

Your life's journey will present many sinful temptations. Resist them. Most everyone wants to go to heaven but doesn't want to give up alluring, sinful conduct. Choose God's way. The gate to heaven is narrow, and only a few will find the narrow road (Matthew 7:13–14). The gate is narrow because it has a particular requirement: acceptance of Jesus Christ as Lord and Savior. *In the game of life, God widely opens the gate to heaven for those who believe and accept Christ.*

NOTES, COMMENTS, OR REFLECTIONS

Make level paths for your feet and take only ways that are firm.
—**PROVERBS 4:26**

*A prudent man sees danger and takes refuge, but
the simple keep going and suffer for it.*
—**PROVERBS 22:3**

*The race is not to the swift, or the battle to the strong, nor
does food come to the wise, or wealth to the brilliant, or favor
to the learned, but time and chance happen to them all.*
—**ECCLESIASTES 9:11**

ATHLETE

Speed kills. So says every coach in just about every sport. Even in an individual sport like golf, swing speed can be an advantage, and not playing fast enough can get you penalized. Speed alone won't win the race. Strength alone won't secure victory.

Speed is a desired skill in most sports, but it must be done in a manner that accommodates teammates, must be within the rules, and must be utilized at the proper time. The fabled metaphor about the race between the rabbit and the turtle emphasizes the importance of focusing on the task at hand. The rabbit ran much faster than the turtle and got so far in front that the rabbit took a nap before crossing the finish line. The plodding turtle stayed on track, passed the rabbit while asleep, and won the race. An athlete should never underestimate an opponent. Speed, focus, and consistency will win most races.

GAME OF LIFE

Before deciding how fast we want to go in life, we must first determine the consequences of going too fast and ignoring life's warning signs. As God points out in the book of Ecclesiastes, the swift doesn't always win the race; nor does the strong always win the battle. Time and circumstances must be given consideration. As we journey through life, we need to make sure we are in the right place at the right time. Timing is as important as speed.

The secret to a happy life is being in the right place at the right time. God will help us with those decisions. God encourages us to pray and seek His will on the major decisions we make in life. He will always be there to help those who love Him. *Life isn't always fair, but God is.* Don't go so fast that you miss seeing the important things in life: Christ, family, friends, weddings, baptisms, christenings, children, and grandchildren. Your life will speed by fast, so stop and smell the roses. In the game of life, let God tell you how fast you need to go.

NOTES, COMMENTS, OR REFLECTIONS

Do nothing out of selfish ambition or vain conceit, but in humility consider others better than yourself. Each of you should look not only to your own interests, but also to the interest of others.
—**PHILIPPIANS 2:3–4**

And let us consider how we may spur one another on toward love and good deeds. Let us not give up meeting together, as some are in the habit of doing, but let us encourage one another—and all the more as you see the Day approaching.
—**HEBREWS 10:24–25**

ATHLETE

Coaches preach "teamwork," selflessness, working for the greater good of the team, putting the team first, and making the team greater than the sum of its parts. Selfish ambition can ruin a team. Genuine humility and putting team goals first produce wins and championships. *Teamwork builds relationships.* Teamwork builds cohesiveness. The more you work together, the more you learn about your teammates' strengths and weaknesses. Teammates motivate each other, learn from each other, and share in the glory of winning. Coaches demand that teammates hold each other accountable. Teamwork is developed by each player putting the team first, communicating with teammates, and sharing responsibilities.

God wants you to work with others as you support a Christian ministry. He wants your Christian team and Christian friends to "shine like stars in the universe" (Philippians 2:15). It takes strength and courage to be a Christian because you will repeatedly face criticism and ridicule from the world. You will be scorned and shunned by people you thought were friends. *Teammates provide strength and protection for those who share the gospel of Jesus Christ.* Teaming up with others who share your faith will make you stronger, and God's protection will make you unbreakable. In the game of life, find your Christian teammates and go share the gospel. At the end of the day, what matters is only what God thinks of you—so there is nothing for your Christian team to fear.

NOTES, COMMENTS, OR REFLECTIONS

30
SPORTS SINS

There are six things the Lord hates; seven that are detestable for Him:
Haughty eyes, a lying tongue, hands that shed innocent
blood, a heart that devises wicked schemes, feet that are
quick to rush to evil, false witness who pours out lies, and
a man who stirs up dissension among brothers.
—**PROVERBS 6:16–19**

And so, I tell you, every sin and blasphemy will be forgiven men,
but the blasphemy against the Spirit will not be forgiven.
—**MATTHEW 12:31**

ATHLETE

Articles have been written about the deadly sins in sports. There is a consensus that the following sports sins are deadly: indifference/apathy, stubbornness, self-doubt, pride, cautions, perfection, and cheating. An athlete's lack of effort, lack of coachability, lack of seriousness, insecurity of performance, and inability to accept constructive criticism will all lead to poor performance and distrust by teammates and coaches. It will also inevitably push the athlete out of the sport. There is a cardinal sin in sports, which is an unforgivable act—"shaving points" to fix the outcome of a game. Gambling in sports has resulted in players, coaches, and referees attempting to fix the outcome by controlling the margin of victory or defeat. This gambling exists in college and professional sports. Shave points, and you will be banned from the sport and could face incarccration.

GAME OF LIFE

The game of life recognizes seven deadly sins: pride, greed, wrath, envy, lust, gluttony, and sloth. God gave Moses the Ten Commandments to keep people from engaging in acts contrary to God's laws. Jesus tells us that all sins are forgivable through the acceptance of Jesus Christ as Savior. The one cardinal and unforgivable sin is the blasphemy of the Holy Spirit. What does this mean? It means that one has specifically rejected God's power and authority through Jesus Christ.

We have all heard the question. How could a loving God condemn someone to eternal damnation? The answer is, He doesn't. When God made man or woman, He gave each a free will to make decisions affecting his or her life. When He gave us Jesus Christ as the Messiah, He provided us with a path to the forgiveness of sin and eternal life in heaven. *Individuals have a choice; they can choose Christ or refuse to choose Him.* If they refuse, then they have chosen, knowing the circumstances and consequences. If they accept Christ, they know the rewards.

All of us sin and will continue to do so until we die. We can have peace about the forgiveness of sin through Jesus Christ. It is the individual's decision that determines where he or she will spend eternity. *Choose Jesus, and you have won the game of life.*

NOTES, COMMENTS, OR REFLECTIONS

31

HOME FIELD ADVANTAGE

Rejoice in the Lord, let your gentleness be evident to all. The Lord is near. Do not be anxious about anything, but in everything, by prayer and petition, with thanksgiving, present your request to God. And the Peace of God, which transcends all understanding, will guard your heart and your minds in Christ Jesus.
—PHILIPPIANS 4:4–7

Children obey your parents in the Lord, for this is right. Honor your father and mother that it may go well with you and that you may enjoy a long life on earth. Father do not exasperate your children. Instead, bring them up in the training and instruction of the Lord.
—EPHESIANS 6:1–4

ATHLETE

In sports, it is believed that the team playing in front of their fans has what is called a "home field advantage." The advantage comes from knowing that most of the fans yelling and screaming in support of the home team are pulling for their success. Visiting teams often use home field advantage as a motivator, knowing that all they have is their teammates and an us-against-them mentality. Opponents love to send the home team and their fans home, feeling dejected. Home teams have a competitive advantage in playing in front of their fans and generally win more games than they lose when playing at home. Referees are frequently accused of being "homers"—that is, giving the home team favorable calls. Most referees, however, are trained to be objective and are not "homers."

GAME OF LIFE

In life, home is where the heart is. It's a place where you feel an emotional attachment. It's where your family and friends reside, a place where you grow up with cherished memories. It is a place you love to return to, no matter how far you have traveled. In the game of life, you get the home field advantage whenever you carry the Lord in your heart. Christ will give you the peace your heart seeks and deserves.

When you have a Christ-centered life, you will always have the comfort of being at home. He will provide you with the emotional, spiritual, and physical blessings needed to have the feeling of home. The greatest blessing is that His crucifixion and resurrection paid for your sins, and once you have accepted them, they will provide you with a home in heaven that lasts for eternity. In the game of life, being a Christian ensures you have a home field advantage forever. Your opponent (the devil) cannot defeat you when you have the home field advantage Christ provides.

NOTES, COMMENTS, OR REFLECTIONS

32
LOSING STREAK

He humbled you, causing you to hunger and then feeding you with manna, which neither you nor your father have known, to teach you that man does not live on bread alone, but on every word that comes from the mouth of the Lord.
—DEUTERONOMY 8:3; MATTHEW 4:4

Therefore, I tell you, do not worry about your life ... who by worrying can add a single hour to your life ... but seek first His Kingdom and His righteousness, and all these things will be given to you ... Do not worry about tomorrow, for tomorrow will worry about itself. Each day has enough trouble of its own.
—MATTHEW 6:25, 27, 33–34

ATHLETE

A losing streak in sports has several different connotations:

a. You can't win a game.
b. You can't win for losing.
c. You can't make the playoffs.
d. You can't win a championship.

A team that loses several games in a row generates feelings unlike any other in sports. Sustained losing tests character, requires reevaluations, and tests the athlete's commitment, but it can also serve as a motivator to turn things around. During losing streaks, coaches throw players under the bus, players blame each other, and fans blame both coaches and players. General wisdom says that if you have losing seasons for a year or two, players are probably at fault. If you have several consecutive losing seasons, players and coaches are at fault; and when you are a perennial loser, management and ownership are at fault. Losing streaks are reversed with more talented players, better coaching, increased commitment, and better preparation. Leaders on teams with losing streaks will step forward and challenge the team to do the things necessary to win.

GAME OF LIFE

Rejecting the Lord will put you on a losing streak from which you will never recover. When you look solely within yourself for your life's purpose, for answers to life's most difficult questions, you aren't likely to get out of your losing streak. If all you think about is money, material possessions, power, immorality, and worldly pleasures, you will never find your purpose in life. The necessities of life are found in those things that lift you emotionally, spiritually, and mentally—things like love, faith, trust, forgiveness, grace, mercy, and making life better for others. In the game of life, it's okay to be successful, to acquire wealth, but you must place your faith and trust in Jesus Christ. God doesn't allow Christians to have losing streaks. God wants you to prosper, and He will provide for your needs. When you stop living on "bread alone" and place your faith and trust in Jesus Christ, seeking His will for your life, you will win the victory in the game of life.

NOTES, COMMENTS, OR REFLECTIONS

33
ERRORS

If any of you is without sin, let him be the first to throw a stone.
—JOHN 8:7

For each of you should carry his own load. A man reaps what he sows.
The one who sows to please his sinful nature will reap destruction;
the one who sows to please the Spirit will reap eternal life.
—GALATIANS 6:5–8

ATHLETE

In sports, an error is a mistake that often has major consequences. The Red Sox sold Babe Ruth to the Yankees for $100,000. Ruth became baseball's greatest home run hitter for the Yankees, and he helped them win four World Series. That was a huge error by the Red Sox. Every NFL team passed over Tom Brady in the draft until the Patriots chose him in the sixth round. After leading the Patriots to six Super Bowl victories, he became the GOAT in the NFL. What a huge error thirty-one NFL teams made!

Players are guilty of errors that cost their team championships. These include dropping a pass in the end zone, permitting a routine ground ball to go through the legs of a fielder, and allowing the winning run to score; these errors have cost teams championships. A missed "gimme putt" cost a golfer a win or, even worse, lost his playing privileges for a while. Passionate fans are quick to cast scorn and ridicule on teams and players who make costly errors.

GAME OF LIFE

In the game of life, everyone makes errors or mistakes. Not all mistakes are sins. We are all quick to throw stones at those who make an error or mistake in life. But we all make mistakes and set ourselves up for scorn and ridicule. *Each person is responsible for his or her actions and shouldn't blame others for his or her errors.*

When your errors impact other people, you should apologize and ask for forgiveness. You should learn from your errors. When you sow seeds of love, kindness, righteousness, forgiveness, patience, integrity, truth, right over wrong, and good over bad, you will reap victory in the game of life and survive any scorn or criticism you receive. If you sow those godly seeds, you will learn from your errors and reap the benefits of what you have sown.

NOTES, COMMENTS, OR REFLECTIONS

34
BAPTISM UNDER FIRE

I, John the Baptist, baptize you with water for repentance. But after me will come one who is more powerful than I, whose sandals I am not fit to carry. He will baptize you with the Holy Spirit and with fire.
—MATTHEW 3:11

Therefore, go and make disciples of all nations, baptizing them in the name of the Father, the Son and the Holy Spirit. And teaching them to obey everything I have commanded you. And surely, I am with you to the very end of age.
—MATTHEW 28:19–20

ATHLETE

The athlete will experience many "baptisms under fire." As the athlete ascends the ladder of sports competitions, he or she will be introduced to a first experience, a new competitive situation in which the athlete will be called on to perform. The athlete's first game at any sports level will present situations that are difficult, unpleasant, and challenging. Preparation, repetition, and self-confidence will help the athlete meet this baptism under fire. Remaining calm, focused, and committed will provide the athlete with the courage to face this baptism under fire.

GAME OF LIFE

In the game of life, one's first encounter with Christ will produce a baptism under fire that will exceed any other earthly experience. When you feel the Holy Spirit beckoning you, you cannot resist. When you realize the sacrifice Jesus made for you on the cross, you will want to accept Him as your Lord and Savior. God rewards those who accept Christ as Lord and Savior. You will experience a love like no other. You will be filled with a passion and desire for love, peace, grace, forgiveness, truth, faith, trust, and hope. You should follow it up with a true baptism as a symbol of your love and acceptance of Jesus and as a symbol that your sins have been washed away and that you have been born again.

NOTES, COMMENTS, OR REFLECTIONS

35
WEAKEST LINK

You cannot hide from God.
—GENESIS 3:8–10

Nothing in all creation is hidden from God's sight.
—HEBREWS 4:13

If you hold to my teachings, you are my disciples. Then, you will know the truth and the truth will set you free.
—JOHN 8:31–32

ATHLETE

A team is often said to be only as strong as its weakest link. If the team's weakest link fails, the team fails. If an opponent successfully exploits the team's weakest link, it will produce victory. Coaches determine the opponent's weakest link, then design a plan of attack around it. Athletes train and prepare so they aren't the team's weakest link. At the end of a close game, a basketball coach will foul the opponent's weakest free throw shooter. A football coach will exploit the opponent's weakest defensive player and attack him or her. A tennis player will take advantage of an opponent's weak backhand. Sports competitions are all about playing to your strengths and to the opponent's weakest link, so athletes should train and prepare themselves to be strong links in the team's chain.

GAME OF LIFE

In the game of life, the devil exploits our weakest link by making sin appealing, pleasurable, desirable, and acceptable. We cannot hide from God. An omnipotent God makes it impossible to hide our sins from Him. We are all sinners. Even after we accept Christ as Savior, we still sin. It's impossible to live our lives without sin.

There is only one way to defeat sin, and that is by accepting Jesus Christ as your Lord and Savior. Once you have done so, all the sin you have ever committed (or will ever commit) is forgiven. God will provide you with the tools you need to live a good and righteous life once you have accepted Christ as Savior. You become the strongest link in any endeavor once you become a Christian. Accept Christ as the Truth, the Life, and the Way; and you will never have to worry about being the weakest link.

NOTES, COMMENTS, OR REFLECTIONS

_____

_____

_____

_____

_____

_____

_____

_____

_____

_____

_____

36
REVENGE

Therefore, rid yourselves of all malice and all deceit, hypocrisy, envy and slander of every kind ... All of you live in harmony with one another; be sympathetic, love as brothers, be compassionate and humble. Do not repay evil with evil or insult with insult, but with blessing.
—1 P ETER 2:1; 3:8–9

It is better, if it is God's will, to suffer for doing good than for doing evil.
—1 P ETER 3:17

Jesus said, "you have heard that it was said "eye for eye' and 'tooth for tooth', but I tell you do not resist an evil person ... Love your enemies and pray for those who persecute you."
—M ATTHEW 5:38, 44

ATHLETE

Players, coaches, and teams are constantly put in a position of playing against an opponent who has defeated them in a previous competition. The previous loss may serve as motivation to seek revenge, to avenge the previous loss by punishing the opponent in the return game. Knowledgeable coaches and experienced players know revenge shouldn't be the motivating factor. Rather, focus, belief in each other, belief in their coaches and their game plan, attention to detail, trust in their system, and practice, practice, practice will sustain the athletes' best efforts to win against the opponent. Revenge as a motivator can lead to poor performance, fighting, cheap shots, and ejection from the game.

GAME OF LIFE

One of the core values of the Christian life is refraining from trying to avenge a wrong that has been done to us. God doesn't want His people to act out of revenge. God tells us to live at peace with everyone, refrain from taking revenge, and leave revenge to God. In the game of life, we don't take revenge against those who have wronged us, but instead, we overcome evil with goodness (Romans 12:18–21). God will take care of those who have wronged us. He will reward those who do the right thing. His goodness and mercy will follow us always.

NOTES, COMMENTS, OR REFLECTIONS

37
SACRIFICE

God is love. This is how God showed His love among us: He sent his one and only Son into the world that we might live through Him. This is love: not that we loved God, but that He loved us and sent His Son as an atoning sacrifice for our sins.
—1 JOHN 4:8–10

But now you must rid yourselves of all such things as these: Anger, rage, malice, slander and filthy language ... As God's chosen people, holy and dearly loved, clothe yourself with compassion, kindness, humility, gentleness and patience.
—COLOSSIANS 3:8, 12

ATHLETE

In the world of sports, sacrifice is a huge component of being successful and winning. The sacrifice fly scores the runner on third base for the winning run. The sacrifice bunt moves the baseball runner into scoring position. The point guard in basketball sacrifices his or her scoring to get teammates more involved in the game. In football, linemen sacrifice their bodies to protect the quarterback and open holes for the running back. Coaches at all levels sacrifice time with their families to focus on coaching and game preparation. Professional athletes frequently sacrifice a portion of their financial remuneration for the sake of the team signing needed players. Sacrifice leads to winning.

GAME OF LIFE

The greatest sacrifice in the history of the world led to the greatest gift ever given. A loving God loved the world so much that He sacrificed His Son, Jesus Christ, to atone for the sins of those who accept Christ as Savior. Why would God do that? Any parent would tell you he or she couldn't sacrifice the life of one of his or her children to save the world. And yet God did precisely that because He loved the world.

God wants to be reconciled with sinful people through Jesus Christ. God wants to give every human being an opportunity to accept Jesus Christ as Savior since it presents the opportunity for sinners to reside in heaven with Him forever. To live in God's grace and receive His forgiveness and mercy should be the goal of every human. You don't have to sacrifice anything, since God did that for you. Accept Christ's sacrifice; put your faith, hope, and trust in the Lord; and give your best effort at living a righteous life. You will claim your victory in the game of life.

NOTES, COMMENTS, OR REFLECTIONS

38
THE SLUMP

Commit to the Lord whatever you do,
and your plans will succeed.
—**PROVERBS 16:3**

Consider it pure joy, my brothers, whenever you face trials of
many kinds, because you know that the testing of your faith
develops perseverance. Perseverance must finish its work so that
you may be mature and complete, not lacking anything.
—**JAMES 1:2–4**

ATHLETE

Every sport, athlete, or team will at some point experiences a slump. Quarterbacks slump in the passing game, baseball players slump in their batting average, and basketball players slump with an inability to score the ball. Teams experience a slump by losing consecutive games or consecutive seasons. A slump is defined as a period when a player or a team isn't performing up to expectations. There are many reasons for a slump, but most of them are mental, not physical. A loss of confidence, an inability to mentally handle failure, anger, and depression can all lead to a prolonged slump.

To get out of a slump, a team or player must get back to a sustained and demonstrated performance. Physically, this may mean doing more repetitions in practice, getting the body in better shape, or practicing harder and longer. Mentally, it starts with changing emotionally, developing a positive attitude, obtaining faith in yourself, raising your self-esteem, increasing your confidence, and receiving encouragement from teammates and coaches. Studying films to educate yourself on what you are doing wrong is important.

GAME OF LIFE

In the game of life, you will experience many slumps. *Every marriage, job, and business experiences one.* Many slumps in life occur due to a lack of money, commitment, faith, trust, or communication. God is prepared to help you out of your slump if you will ask with faith and reverence. God wants to prosper His people. Having a childlike faith means truly believing in what you are seeking and having faith in God to deliver. Children are trusting by nature. They have an innocence God loves.

Don't be afraid to ask God for His help. Place your faith in His response. Just as an athlete studies films to end his or her slump, so, too, should we study the Bible to help us get out of our slump. *Faith in God will give you the perseverance you need to break out of your slump.*

NOTES, COMMENTS, OR REFLECTIONS

39

STEALING A BASE

You shall not steal.
—Exodus 20:15

Do not give the devil a foothold. He who has been stealing must steal no longer, but must work, doing something useful with his own hands, that he may have something to share with those in need.
—Ephesians 4:27–28

The Lord said to Moses, "If anyone sins and is unfaithful to the Lord by deceiving his neighbor about something entrusted to him or left in his care or stolen. He must return what was entrusted to him or was stolen … He must make restitution in full …
—Leviticus 6:2–5

ATHLETE

In baseball, stealing home base is a monumental achievement that is seldom performed successfully. Stealing any base is a positive for the team at bat because it improves the chances of scoring a run on a base hit. Hall of Fame player Ty Cobb performed one of the greatest base-stealing events in baseball. He stole second, third, and home base in the same inning and in four separate games. Stealing home base is comparable to a hole-in-one in golf, a one-hundred-yard kickoff return in football, and a length-of-the-court basket in basketball. All these are rare feats that are positive for the home team. Stealing can be inappropriate in baseball; that's when the home team uses a camera to steal a catcher's pitch sign to the pitcher and instantly relays that information to the batter by some signal. This isn't allowed and subjects the team and players to punishment.

GAME OF LIFE

In the game of life, stealing what belongs to someone else is a sin. It violates God's commandments. God wants everyone to work, earn, and share his or her blessings. Stealing requires restitution in full. Never take something that isn't yours unless you have permission from the owner or the one in lawful possession. Stealing may be caused by jealousy, low self-esteem, depression, or a lack of acceptance by peers. Don't let worldly ways cause you to steal, lie, or cheat. God wants you to come to Him for your needs and requests. He will take care of you. And in so doing, God will steal your heart, mind, and soul. There is one form of stealing we all endure or accept; that's when someone steals our hearts with his or her love. *God's love has stolen the hearts of Christians.*

NOTES, COMMENTS, OR REFLECTIONS

40
TEAM CULTURE

If you have any encouragement from being united with Christ, if any comfort from His love, if any fellowship with the Spirit, if any tenderness and compassion, then make joy complete, by being like-minded, having the same love, being one in spirit and purpose. Do nothing out of selfish ambition or vain conceit, but in humility consider others better than yourselves. Each of you should look not only to your own interest, but also the interest of others.
—PHILIPPIANS 2:1–4

Whoever wants to become great among you must be your servant, and whoever wants to be first must be slave of all. For even the Son of Man did not come to be served, but to serve, and to give his life as a ransom for many.
—MARK 10:43–45

ATHLETE

Team culture is one of the most important concepts in team sports. A new coach hired to turn around a losing program will initially talk about changing the team culture. A team's culture sets the expectations for how players will behave on and off the playing field. Coaches want a team culture that produces a feeling of "one for all and all for one." This is a team whose players look on one another as brothers or sisters. Your team's culture is its identity.

Coaches want a team whose players care more about the team than about themselves. A player becomes a cancer to the team when he or she puts individual goals above team goals. Leaders on teams are those who promote a positive team culture. A winning team culture is produced by having positive attitudes, doing hard work, sacrificing individual goals for team goals, providing leadership, sharing or caring, and consistently demonstrating performance.

GAME OF LIFE

In the game of life, Christians are called on to promote a culture of service, love, sharing, forgiveness, grace, and honesty. A Christian team culture looks beyond selfish interests for the benefit of others. A Christian team culture requires sacrifice and service, patience and understanding, love and trust, righteousness and forgiveness, humbleness and humility. A Christian culture epitomizes "Just win, baby" in its fight for one's soul. These aren't words but actions that produce a Christian culture. Surround yourself with people who share your Christian values and use your team to point lost souls to the cross for redemption and salvation. In doing so, you score another victory in the game of life.

NOTES, COMMENTS, OR REFLECTIONS

41
HAVE FUN

Put your hope in God, who richly provides us
with everything for our enjoyment.
—1 TIMOTHY 6:17

I tell you there will be more rejoicing in Heaven over one sinner who
repents than over ninety-nine righteous persons who do not need to repent.
—LUKE 15:7

For the wages of sin is death, but the gift of God is
eternal life through Jesus Christ our Lord.
—ROMANS 6:23

ATHLETE

Every sport has winners and losers. Planning, preparation, execution, focus, and sometimes luck play a huge role in winning. The lack thereof is likely to produce losing. Winning and losing are inevitable. The "fun" in sports is found in competing. Sports events are meant to be mirthful—joyous, cheerful, and merry. They are meant for enjoyment and entertainment. Grade school, junior high, and high school sports are to be enjoyed and filled with fun, making lifetime memories.

Coaches at all levels will frequently tell their players to "go have fun" as a part of their last-minute pep talk. Competing is fun. Excelling is fun. Participating is fun. Winning is fun. Even losing players have fun and probably learn more about themselves than from winning experiences. If you aren't having fun playing sports, then find another form of recreation. Find laughter and humor in sports participation.

GAME OF LIFE

In the game of life, you are born and will die. In between those two events, you live. How you live your life determines where you will spend your afterlife. God wants you to have a life filled with joy, fun, laughter, and love. A Christian's definition of fun doesn't include the use of drugs, immoral behavior, or getting drunk on alcohol. It doesn't include harmful gossip. It doesn't include illegal conduct. Sinful behavior isn't fun, and its consequences are devastating.

There is a wealth of wholesome, healthy forms of entertainment for all people. Find friends who like to have good fun. Once you have accepted Christ as Savior and repented of your sins, you will be amazed by the enjoyment, entertainment, and fun He will provide. You can live life without fear and with the blessing of God, and upon death, you can experience the greatest fun location ever devised—heaven. So go, *have fun*, and claim another victory.

NOTES, COMMENTS, OR REFLECTIONS

42

GET THE BALL ROLLING

The Apostle Paul (a/k/a Saul) was still breathing murderous threats against the Lord's disciples ... Jesus suddenly appeared and said to him, "Saul, why do you persecute me? I am Jesus whom you are persecuting. Now get up and go into the city and you will be told what to do.
—ACTS 9:1-6

Saul said, "it is to us that this message of salvation has been sent ... I want you to know that through Jesus, the forgiveness of sins is proclaimed to you. Through Him everyone who believes is justified from everything you could not be justified from by the law of Moses.
—ACTS 13:26, 38-39

ATHLETE

"Get the ball rolling" is a sports metaphor that means to start the action and make the opening move. In golf, you make a putt when you get the ball rolling. In football, the game begins with the kickoff. The jump ball starts the ball rolling in basketball. The metaphor can also refer to an athlete who is beginning his or her career. Many athletes will describe themselves as nervous or anxious until the ball gets rolling. Once the game begins, then the nerves disappear, and they can focus on execution.

GAME OF LIFE

Jesus Christ is the reason for Christianity. Apart from Jesus, no person played a more historical role in the development of Christianity than the apostle Paul. Paul had been a persecutor of those who followed Jesus. He was on his way to Damascus when Jesus confronted him. Jesus not only stopped Paul's persecution but also asked him to get the ball rolling for Christianity. Paul accepted this challenge and went throughout the region, preaching the gospel of Jesus Christ. His extensive writings make up a substantial part of the New Testament.

In the game of life, individuals get the ball rolling toward a Christian life when they personally meet Christ through the Holy Spirit. Life is never the same for one who gets the ball rolling toward a life of godly love, trust, faith, and service. God wants you to believe in Christ, accept His salvation, and then get the ball rolling by sharing the good news of the gospel. *The good news is eternal life in heaven through Jesus Christ.*

NOTES, COMMENTS, OR REFLECTIONS

43
STEP UP TO THE PLATE

All men will hate you because of Me, but he who stands firm to the end will be saved.
—**MATTHEW 10:22–23**

Jesus said, "It is written, worship the Lord your God and serve Him only."
—**LUKE 4:8**

ATHLETE

Every athlete must accept responsibility for his or her actions. An athlete steps up to the plate when he or she rises to the occasion and performs for the benefit of the team. Stepping up to the plate requires an athlete to recognize the significance of the moment, accept responsibility for embracing the moment, and perform to the best of his or her ability. An athlete won't always be successful in those situations, but all anyone can ask is that the athlete give his or her best effort. *It takes courage and strength to embrace the moment in stepping up to the plate.*

GAME OF LIFE

In the game of life, Christians step up to the plate not only by worshipping and serving God but also by sharing the Christian faith with nonbelievers. It takes courage and strength to confront sinners who have little interest in Christianity.

If you step up to the plate, you will be mocked, ridiculed, and made fun of, but in the end, you will convert many nonbelievers into seeking Christ. God will give you the strength and courage to witness for Him; all you must do is ask Him. God wants to commune with His followers. He wants to provide them with all they need to help bring righteousness and goodness into the world. Incorporating God's will, His commandments, and His purpose into your physical and mental activities is stepping up to the plate. When you do so, you claim another victory.

NOTES, COMMENTS, OR REFLECTIONS

44
TIME-OUT

Then the Lord said to Moses … "remember the sabbath by keeping it holy … you must observe my Sabbaths. This will be a sign between you and me for the generations to come, so you may know that I am the Lord, who makes you holy."
—Exodus 20:8; 32:12–13

And on the seventh day, God rested from all His work.
—Hebrews 4:4

Come to me all you who are weary and burdened, and I will give you rest.
—Matthew 11:28

ATHLETE

Time-outs are important in sports. They can be used to break an opponent's momentum. They can be used to allow the athlete time to think, reflect, rest, relax, replenish fluids, and get coaching advice. Coaches use time-outs not only to discuss strategy but also to inspire the team to give greater effort. Time-outs are used to stop the clock from running and extend the game. Knowing when and how to use time-outs is important for both the athlete and coach because most sports have a limit on time-outs. Coaches, teachers, and parents have been known to use time-outs as a punishment for a misbehaving youth.

GAME OF LIFE

Life moves at a hectic pace. Education, homework, chores, work, social engagements, mortgages, taxes, children, marriages, debt, injury, illness, and loss of a loved one can make life seem difficult at times. One can be overwhelmed by both the mental and physical demands of life. In the game of life, taking time-outs is important to the health and well-being of everyone. Families take a time-out when they go on family vacations.

Christians use their time-outs to pray, asking God for help, guidance, strength, and support. We seek God's power and support to alleviate the stresses and pressures daily life presents. It isn't uncommon for many people to seek and find God during the most broken times in their lives. He provides reassurance and strength to move forward. *So take your time-outs daily and set aside special time to commune with the Lord. The results will amaze you!*

NOTES, COMMENTS, OR REFLECTIONS

All scripture is God breathed and is useful for teaching, rebuking, correcting, and training in righteousness, so that the man of God may be thoroughly equipped for every good work.
—2 TIMOTHY 3:16–17

Train yourself to be Godly, for physical training is of some value, but Godliness has value for all things, holding promise for both the present life and the life to come.
—1 TIMOTHY 4:8

ATHLETE

An ace in the hole in sports is generally considered an advantage or resource an athlete possesses that, when used in a timely manner, propels him or her to victory. The term originated from the game of poker, where one of the competitors holds an ace, the highest-rated card, in a downward position, waiting for the prime opportunity to play it. An ace in the hole presents a winning opportunity. Advantages held in reserve until needed constitute an ace in the hole.

GAME OF LIFE

In the game of life, the Christian's ace in the hole is the Bible. The Bible equips us to do good, be good, live righteously, love others, share blessings, and make life better for others—all done to the glory and praise of our Lord and Savior, Jesus Christ. God gave us scripture to use to our advantage.

Every facet of our lives is addressed in the Bible. God's love, grace, and mercy permeate the Bible.

Accepting Christ as Savior gives us an ace in the hole for us to play when needed most. God loves to communicate with His people. He gave us the Bible to help us communicate with Him and share His good news. He responds to our prayers to let us know He is listening. When your heart holds God the Father, Jesus Christ the Son, and the Holy Spirit, you have a Holy Trinity. *That is your ace in the hole, the highest card anyone could ever hold with the ability to defeat anything and everything thrown at you.*

NOTES, COMMENTS, OR REFLECTIONS

46
STRIKEOUT

He who conceals his sins does not prosper, but whosoever confesses and renounces them finds mercy.
—**PROVERBS 28:13**

Pride goes before destruction, a haughty spirit before a fall.
—**PROVERBS 16:18**

The fear of the Lord leads to life; then one rests content; untouchable by trouble.
—**PROVERBS 19:23**

ATHLETE

Babe Ruth is considered one of the greatest home run hitters of all time. His career record for home runs (714) stood for many years until Hank Aaron broke it. But little is written or said about the 1,330 times he struck out. He is remembered for his successes, not his failures. *He was not afraid to strike out.* He wasn't afraid of momentary failure. He had confidence in his abilities, which weren't shaken by his numerous strikeouts. All athletes will fail more than they succeed. Great athletes learn from their strikeouts and use them as motivation for success.

GAME OF LIFE

We will all strike out in life. We will experience failure. We will engage in sinful conduct. In the game of life, Christians fear the Lord. This fear negates all other fears, including the failures we experience and the sins we commit. God wants us to prosper. He wants us to succeed. He wants us to enjoy victory. He wants us to expend our best efforts. But when we fail, when we sin, *He wants us to confess our strikeouts to Him.* Forgiveness and mercy await those who repent and seek God's mercy. Christians depend on their faith and look to the Lord for strength and perseverance. God grants His grace and mercy to all who seek Him and His forgiveness. God will never stop loving you.

NOTES, COMMENTS, OR REFLECTIONS

*Whatever happens, conduct yourselves in a
manner worthy of the Gospel of Christ.*
—PHILIPPIANS 1:27

*A man's wisdom gives him patience; it is to
his glory to overlook an offense.*
—PROVERBS 19:11

Man is destined to die once, and after that to face judgment.
—HEBREWS 9:27

*In Christ we have redemption through His blood, the forgiveness
of sins, in accordance with the riches of God's grace that He
lavished on us with all wisdom and understanding.*
—EPHESIANS 1:7–8

ATHLETE

Every individual who has played a round of golf understands the term *mulligan*. It means taking an extra golf shot after the first shot is poorly struck or positioned. When you hit a mulligan and it turns out better than your first shot, you count the mulligan on your scorecard. It is believed the term originated from a caddie named Mulligan; when playing, he liked to have a second chance at hitting his first shot on the first tee. The rules of golf don't allow mulligans. Rather, you play and count every shot—no mulligans. In some sports like track and swimming, athletes get a mulligan if they make a false start at the beginning of the race.

GAME OF LIFE

None of us are perfect. Only one person who walked the face of this earth was perfect—Jesus Christ. And He was crucified for His preaching and teaching. Because of our imperfections, we all need a mulligan in our lives. We need a second chance to start over, learn from our failures, and seek a path that will make us better human beings.

In the game of life, Jesus Christ provides us with our mulligan. Accepting Christ as Savior and making Him Lord of our lives give us our do-over. Our sins are forgiven. As we develop our relationship with Christ through prayer, Bible study, and meditation, we realize our scorecard is clean and that we need to pursue a life filled with love, kindness, goodness, and righteousness. *There is no mulligan or second chance after you die.*

NOTES, COMMENTS, OR REFLECTIONS

48

CRITICISM

Be merciful, just as your Father is merciful.
—LUKE 6:36

*Do not judge and you will not be judged. Do not condemn and
you will not be condemned. Forgive and you will be forgiven.
Give, and it will be given to you. A good measure, pressed down,
shaken together and running over will be poured into your lap.
For with the measure you use, it will be measured to you.*
—LUKE 6:37–38

ATHLETE

Anyone who participates in sports or sporting events is going to receive criticism. It may be positive as in critical acclaim (turning in an outstanding performance), but more than likely, it will be negative (failure to perform). Criticism is part of sports. Coaches encourage players to "try harder," "do better," and "make a play." Negative criticism will come from fans, sports writers, and broadcast journalists. Social media has introduced a whole new genre of sports critics. Great athletes can use negative criticism as a motivating factor to improve performance. They also can block out negative comments.

GAME OF LIFE

Christianity has long been criticized as a faith of violence, corruption, bigotry, homophobia, and abuse of women's rights. Many things have been said and done in the name of Christianity. *Such criticisms aren't warranted.*

God tells us to love each other and love Him. The Christian faith is based on love.

In the game of life, we as Christians have an obligation—indeed, a commandment—to love, forgive, aid, support, comfort, and pray for those whose actions are contrary to God's teachings. Leave judgment and criticism to God. In the game of life, we pray as Christians for forgiveness. We pray for sinners to repent and develop a clean mind and pure heart for the Lord. No one is without sin in his or her life. *Focus on removing sin from your life and pray that others will do the same. And always remember that Christ died for sinners.*

NOTES, COMMENTS, OR REFLECTIONS

49

ABILITY OR TALENT

From everyone who has been given much, much will be demanded; and from the one who has been entrusted with much, much more will be asked.
—LUKE 12:48

I urge you to live a life worthy of the calling you have received. Be completely humble and gentle; be patient, bearing with one another in love ... There is one body, one faith, one baptism, one God and Father for all, who is over all, and through all and in all.
—EPHESIANS 4:1–5

We have different gifts, according to the grace given us. If a man's gift is prophesying, let him use it in proportion to his faith. If it is serving, let him serve. if it is teaching, let him teach; if it is encouraging, let him encourage; If it is contributing to the needs of others, let him give generously; If it is leadership, let him govern diligently. If it is showing mercy, let him do it cheerfully.
—ROMANS 12:6–8

ATHLETE

We often hear the term "God-given talent or ability." It refers to a talent or ability that is innate, not learned. It is so extraordinary that it could come only from a higher power. Many famous and successful athletes have been described as having been given a talent by God. These athletes recognize their God-given talents and put in the time and effort to utilize such talent and ability to make them special. Michael Jordan, LeBron James, Serena

Williams, Tiger Woods, Tom Brady, Wayne Gretzky, and Babe Zaharias are individuals who excelled in the sports arena and on the playing field. Most all athletes who have been anointed with God-given talent will tell you that at the very heart of those who have such an ability is whether they have the inner desire to push themselves, practice long and hard, maximize their talent, and reach their potential.

GAME OF LIFE

In the game of life, God equips us with spiritual gifts. The Holy Spirit gives us wisdom, understanding, counsel, fortitude, piety, and fear of the Lord. Search for your God-given talent and ability. Ask God to show you His spiritual gifts. Ask Christian friends to tell you what they see as God's gift to you. Look for gifts in adversity. Find your joy in God's word. Make life better for others. Seek God's will in your life. In 1 Timothy 5:9, God tells us not to neglect our spiritual gifts, to train ourselves to be godly (1 Timothy 4:7), and to do everything in love (1 Corinthians 16:4). Christians utilize their God-given talents and abilities to benefit others as well as themselves.

NOTES, COMMENTS, OR REFLECTIONS

50
FALL FROM GRACE

You who are trying to be justified by the law have been alienated from Christ; you have fallen away from Grace. But by faith we eagerly await through the Spirit the righteousness for which we hope. For in Christ the only thing that counts is faith expressing itself through love.
—GALATIANS 5:4–6

The righteousness from God comes through faith in Jesus Christ to all who believe. For all have sinned and fall short of the Glory of God and are justified freely by His grace through the redemption that came from Jesus Christ.
—ROMANS 3:22–24

ATHLETE

Sports history is full of athletes who, having reached the pinnacle of their profession, fall from grace. For these individuals the scandal that caused their fall from grace is dramatic, sometimes career ending, and it was almost always brought about by some sinful conduct. Bicyclists who admit to doping during the Tour de France, home run hitters who admit to taking steroids, and track athletes stripped of their medals for using performance-enhancing drugs are examples of scandals leading to a fall from grace. Virtually every sport has athletes who by their conduct engaged in scandalous behavior that stripped them of their wins or medals. The question is why. Why would someone who has fame, fortune, God-given talent, and a beautiful family risk it all by engaging in illicit conduct? The answer varies with the athlete, but at the root of such failures is a feeling of entitlement, greed, a lack of discipline, an abuse of power, a lack of conscience, jealousy, a fear of failure, and a lack of self-respect.

GAME OF LIFE

In the game of life, we recognize we are all going to experience failure. We are all going to commit some act that is senseless or scandalous. We are all going to fall from grace at some time. How we handle that failure will define us. The way Christians overcome scandal or failure is to renew and recommit to their faith by placing their hope and trust in the Lord, by seeking forgiveness. When we seek God's will in our lives, He will protect us and help us avoid repeating failed conduct. Christians recognize the need to conduct themselves according to God's commandments. Sometimes, however, we either forget or ignore those commandments. When we conduct ourselves with honesty, truth, repentance, humbleness, respect, and discipline, God forgives us and extends His grace and mercy to us. God restores us to a place that exceeds any pinnacle we may have reached. Don't miss *the most important day of your life. The most important decision you will ever make is to accept Christ as Savior, make Him the Lord of your life, and seek His will daily.*

NOTES, COMMENTS, OR REFLECTIONS

51

WINNING ATTITUDE

Those people honor me with their lips, but their hearts are far from me ... What comes out of the mouth makes him unclean ... The things that come out of the mouth, come from the heart.
—MATTHEW 15:8, 11, 18

Whatever is true, whatever is noble, whatever is right, whatever is lovely, whatever is admirable—if anything is excellent or praiseworthy—think about such things.
—PHILIPPIANS 4:8

ATHLETE

Coaches have preached for years that a winning attitude is essential to establishing a winning culture. Yogi Berra, the Hall of Fame Yankee baseball legend, once said, "Baseball is 90 percent mental, and the other half is physical." A winning attitude is essential to sustained success. Mental thoughts reflect actions. Physical actions reflect our thoughts. Personal athletic achievement is greatly influenced by the athlete's attitude. A winning attitude evolves from demonstrated performance. Demonstrated performance evolves from physical and mental preparation. Physical and mental preparation evolve as much from what an athlete does off the field as from the playing field. Once the athlete is physically and mentally prepared, the on-field performance will lead to victory. Victory leads to a winning attitude that, in turn, leads to a winning culture.

GAME OF LIFE

A Christian's winning attitude evolves from his or her relationship with the Lord. Knowing Christ as Savior and as Lord of your life, sustaining your faith and loyalty to Christ, will lead you to do what is right, good, kind, loving, and forgiving. God is much more interested in what your actions are than in the words that come out of your mouth. Our actions reflect our hearts and demonstrate our true beliefs. Evil acts, cursing, immorality, and cheating reflect an unclean heart. Cursing accomplishes nothing. It's a sign of weakness. May the words that come out of your mouth and the actions you undertake be acceptable to our Lord and Savior. In the game of life, play with a winning attitude, and Christ will honor you with a victory.

NOTES, COMMENTS, OR REFLECTIONS

52
ON THE ROPES

*Do not be afraid. Stand firm and you will see the
deliverance the Lord will bring to you today.*
—EXODUS 14:10

But the Lord stood at my side and gave me strength.
—2 TIMOTHY 4:17

*The Lord will rescue me from every evil attack and will bring
me safely to His Heavenly Kingdom. To Him be the glory forever
and ever … The Lord be with your spirit. Grace be with you.*
—2 TIMOTHY 4:18, 22

ATHLETE

Being "on the ropes" is a sports metaphor referring to an athlete on the verge of defeat. A boxer is forced against the ropes when he or she is constantly being pounded with no clear escape path. The blows of the opponent keep the boxer against the ropes; if he doesn't get free, he will suffer defeat. A marathon runner, whose legs are collapsing and thighs are burning, is on the ropes. A coach who can't produce winning seasons is said to be on the ropes. Being on the ropes requires action to avoid defeat. It takes strength to release one who is on the ropes.

GAME OF LIFE

In the game of life, we will all find ourselves on the ropes, headed for defeat if we are unable to get off the ropes. Christ is the one who will deliver you from defeat. He will provide you with the strength to free you from the ropes. In life, everyone will face challenges, be it alcohol, drugs, sex, peer pressures, marital difficulties, or financial issues, knowing that defeat is certain if we don't act. Turn to God, and He will stand firm with you. He will stand at your side and give you strength. He will rescue you and bring you off the ropes and safely into His presence.

NOTES, COMMENTS, OR REFLECTIONS

*No eye has seen, no ear has heard, no mind has conceived
what God has prepared for those who love Him.*
—1 CORINTHIANS 2:9

Do not let your hearts be troubled and do not be afraid.
—JOHN 14:27

*In his heart, a man plans his course, but
the Lord determines the steps.*
—PROVERBS 16:9

*For I know the plans I have for you, declares
the Lord, plans to prosper you and not to harm
you, plans to give you hope and a future.*
—JEREMIAH 29:11

ATHLETE

Analytics have become a big part of sports. Universities offer degrees in sports analytics. Sports analytics are the analysis of sports data to determine player performance or recruitment to make in-game decisions (for example, should I go for it on the fourth down or kick a field goal?) or develop a game plan. Coaches use analytics to determine the likelihood of success. Analytics are used to make prognostications. Baseball uses analytics to tell how players perform in certain situations. It is used heavily in the planning process for athletic competition in almost every sport.

GAME OF LIFE

God the Father; Jesus Christ, our Savior; and the Holy Spirit are part of the Holy Trinity, which serves as our Analyst. God has a plan for the life of individuals. Seek His plan and follow His will. He has a path to success for those who have accepted Christ as Savior. The Holy Spirit will guide you in carrying out God's plan for your life. God examines your thoughts, actions, and words. He hears your prayers and requests for help. He measures your faith, righteousness, and goodness by your actions. He knows the sincerity of your heart. He knows whether you love Him and, if so, how much. In the game of life, Christians win when God's analysis finds them faithful in their beliefs and conduct.

NOTES, COMMENTS, OR REFLECTIONS

PRAYER AT SPORTING EVENTS

*Trust in the Lord with all your heart and lean not on
your own understanding. In all your ways, acknowledge
Him, and He will make your paths straight.*
—PROVERBS 3:5–6

*Everyone who competes in the games goes into training.
They do it to get a crown that will not last, but we
do it to get a crown that will last forever.*
—1 CORINTHIANS 9:25

*I was pushed back and about to fall, but the Lord helped me. The
Lord is my strength, and my song. He has become my salvation.*
—PSALM 118:13–14

ATHLETE

The US Supreme Court ruled in June of 2022 that a football coach at a public high school couldn't be fired for engaging in prayer following a game. Previous judicial decisions ruled that students at public schools couldn't be coerced into participating in group prayers at sporting events. The Supreme Court's ruling allowing prayer was based on the First Amendment to the US Constitution, the right of religious freedom. Christian pro athletes will frequently meet at center court or midfield after a game and offer thanks to God. Informal and voluntary prayers can be utilized before or after games in the exercise of the right of religious freedom.

GAME OF LIFE

In the game of life, an individual can say prayers before or after any event. Sports competitions can be stressful. Prayer helps to calm the athlete and individual. Prayers to get help, to find protection from injury, to express thanks for the blessings of life, and to find grace for your competitors are all legitimate reasons for prayer. But the greatest reason to pray is to give praise, glory, and thanks for the blessing of Jesus Christ. Prayer equips every individual with a foundational tool necessary to seek God's will, blessings, and protection. Pray that God will let you play well but fairly.

Pray that competition will strengthen you but not make you hostile. Ask God to humble you in victory and to be gracious in defeat. Ask the Lord to see you not when you are cheered but when you bend to help your opponent up.

Let victory bring you joy and losing keep you from envy. Ask the Lord to remind you that sports events are just games. *And most of all, ask the Lord to help you be a good example to other athletes and individuals, and conduct yourself in a manner that brings praise and glory to Jesus.*

NOTES, COMMENTS, OR REFLECTIONS

Therefore, stand firm. Let nothing move you. Always give yourselves fully to the work of the Lord, because you know that your labor in the Lord is not in vain.
—1 CORINTHIANS 15:58

Those who have served well, gain an excellent standing and great assurance in their faith in Christ Jesus.
—1 TIMOTHY 3:13

Well done, good and faithful servant! You have been faithful with a few things; I will put you in charge of many things. Come and share your Master's happiness.
—MATTHEW 25:21

But as for you, be strong and do not give up, for your work will be rewarded.
—2 CHRONICLES 15:7

ATHLETE

The road to success in sports begins with a desire and commitment to be the best at something. Successful teams and athletes are those who seek to be extraordinary. The successful athlete and teams are those who have the biggest hearts, the most commitment, and the desire to excel. Hard work and teamwork are essential to success. A famous athlete once said that the only place you will ever find success before work is in the dictionary. The most successful athletes and teams are those who have a daily and regular routine consisting of hard practices, repetition, commitment, and desire.

Successful athletes and teams have an abundance of determination and teamwork. Evaluations should be done honestly without excuses.

GAME OF LIFE

The game of life mirrors the games of athletes and teams. A big heart for the Lord, hard work to overcome obstacles, determination to live and walk in faith, self-sacrifice for the glory of the Lord, and teamwork with other Christians all lead to living life as a successful Christian. Christians must be doers of the word, not just hearers (James 1:22–25). *Believers must equip themselves with love, joy, peace, gentleness, goodness, faithfulness, self-discipline, sharing, and self-sacrifice.*

Loving the Lord is easy, but sharing His message will present obstacles. Christians truly achieve success when they care more about offending God than about offending the world, when they care more about pleasing God than about pleasing themselves or others, and when they give God the credit and glory for accomplishments. Success and hard work go together in sports and the game of life.

NOTES, COMMENTS, OR REFLECTIONS

*He who belongs to God hears what God says. The reason
you do not hear is that you do not belong to God.*
—JOHN 8:47

*No one will be able to stand against you all the days of your
life. As I was with Moses, so I will be with you. I will never
leave you nor forsake you. Be strong and courageous.*
—JOSHUA 1:5–6

*But the Lord stood at my side and gave me strength … the Lord
will rescue me from every evil attack and will bring me safely to
His Heavenly Kingdom. To Him be glory forever and ever.*
—2 TIMOTHY 4:17–18

ATHLETE

Sports continuously present challenges. Racism; COVID-19; financial concerns; the abuse of performance-enhancing drugs; athlete abuse, social media attacks; playing time; team cuts; free agency; name, image, and likeness issues; bad referees; and fan intimidation—the list of challenges goes on and on. Even youth sports have challenges, including meddling parents, who won't let the game belong to the kids; athletes who refuse to own their performances or decisions; a lack of respect between coaches and players; a failure to protect youths from injury; and too much emphasis on winning and not enough on participation, development, and having fun. Meeting the challenges can prove difficult, costly, and time consuming. For the sake of the athlete, the team, and the sport, these challenges must be met.

GAME OF LIFE

Perhaps athletes, teams, and sports organizations could learn lessons from the Christians' game of life. God commands that we love our neighbors as ourselves. The Bible tells us to love and pray for our adversaries. Christians seek to make life better for others and to share our blessings. We perform to bring praise and glory to God first and not to ourselves. Sports events at any level are just games. Christians meet challenges with right thinking, honesty, passion, goodwill, and concern for the welfare of others. Christians meet challenges with faith and belief in God's love, grace, and mercy. Because we know God is with us, we must meet challenges head-on without fear. If God is for us, who can be against us (Romans 8:31)?

NOTES, COMMENTS, OR REFLECTIONS

*God created man in his own image; in the image of God,
He created him; Male and female He created them.*
—**GENESIS 1:27**

*A new command I give you: that you Love one another. As
I have loved you, you also are to love one another.*
—**JOHN 13:34**

*Peter began to speak: "I now realize how true it is that
God does not show favoritism, but accepts men from
every nation who fear Him and do what is right.*
—**ACTS 10:34–35**

ATHLETE

The world has come a long way in improving racial relationships. Sporting events have played an integral part in breaking down the barriers between races and improving relationships among ethnic groups. There is much left to be done to eliminate racism in sports. Racism, ethnic prejudice, and discrimination based on race have no place in any sport or in the world. And yet they still exist. Athletes of all races continue to help sports eliminate these prejudices. It begins with youth sports, where all that matters is playing the sport, getting to know your teammates, rooting for your teammates, learning to be friends, learning to share cultures, and learning to judge someone by his or her character rather than by his or her skin color.

GAME OF LIFE

In the game of life, there should be no discrimination whatsoever. God made us all in His image. God has no color, gender, or prejudices. God has love for all. We may not agree with some aspects of someone else's life, but God commands that we love that person and pray for him or her—and not judge him or her. God shows no partiality. He expects us to do the same. *God loves all races, and He expects us to do the same.* God forgives us of our trespasses and commands us to do the same. Let's all make a pledge that we are going to eliminate racism and gender bias, and that such conduct has no place in sports or in the world.

NOTES, COMMENTS, OR REFLECTIONS

Whoever does God's will is my brother, my sister and my mother.
—**MARK 3:35**

Jesus said, "because you have seen me, you have believed; blessed are those who have not seen and yet have believed".
—**JOHN 20:29**

The apostle Paul said, "I pray that you may be active in sharing your faith, so that you will have a full understanding of every good thing we have in Christ."
—**PHILEMON 1:6–7**

ATHLETE

The unsung heroes in sports are those who serve as staff to support the endeavors of the team and its athletes. Scouts, trainers, equipment managers, locker room attendants, secretaries, ticket personnel, security staff, and human resources personnel are just a few who serve in jobs to assist the team and its athletes in being successful, healthy, and informed. They are there to meet their needs. They work in unison to make life better and easier for players, coaches, and fans. Their efforts should be recognized and appreciated by the team and athletes.

GAME OF LIFE

Many individuals supported the ministry of Jesus Christ, resulting in the creation of the Christian faith. The twelve disciples; John the Baptist; the apostle Paul; Timothy; Jesus's earthly father, Joseph; His brother James; and His mother, Mary, all saw Jesus, recognized He was God in the flesh, and supported His mission. The Christian religion has grown massively because of millions of people who never saw Christ but had faith in Him and His message and were willing to share His message. In the game of life, it is incumbent on believers to share the gospel, the good news that Christ died for their sins, that He rose again, and that through Him there is reconciliation with God and life eternal in heaven. When you accept Christ as Savior, you become part of His support staff and have an obligation to share the news of His love, grace, mercy, and redemption.

NOTES, COMMENTS, OR REFLECTIONS

*All who are skilled among you are to come and
make everything the Lord has commanded.*
—EXODUS 35:10

*Those who have served well, gain an excellent standing
and great assurance in their faith in Jesus Christ.*
—1 TIMOTHY 3:13

*Live a life worthy of the calling you have received. Be completely
humble and gentle; be patient, bearing with one another in love …
There is one body, one spirit … one Lord, one faith, one baptism, one
God and Father of all, who is over all and through all and in all.*
—EPHESIANS 4:1–4

ATHLETE

Athletic ability is acquired in different ways. Many athletes are born with God-given athletic ability. They have excellent speed, agility, size, and coordination—abilities God naturally gave to them. They gravitate to the sport that best utilizes their God-given ability. Most athletes acquire their abilities through hard work, practice, preparation, repetition, weight training, and physical and mental exercises. Whether their athletic ability is God given or made by man or woman's efforts, successful athletes possess certain innate traits: passion for their sport, perseverance, commitment, discipline, and a strong work ethic. They use their abilities to seek victory, pursue glory, and achieve success to assist the success of their team.

Christians likewise possess abilities to serve the Lord. All of them are God given. *It is the responsibility of each person who accepts Jesus Christ as Savior to recognize his or her abilities and how best to utilize them for serving the glory of God to others.* Some possess musical abilities, some possess oratorical abilities, some have writing skills, and many have leadership abilities. All can be used to further the cause of Christianity. And then many have little or no ability but a great passion for Christ and His ministry. They have great, unconditional faith which, when shared, serves up glory to the Lord. In the game of life, use your abilities to *serve* the gospel of Jesus Christ and bring Him glory.

NOTES, COMMENTS, OR REFLECTIONS

EXTRA INNINGS AND OVERTIME

*The Kingdom of Heaven is near. Repent
and believe the good news.*
—MARK 1:15

*I urge you to abstain from sinful desires which war against your soul.
Live such good lives ... that, though they accuse you of doing wrong,
they may see your good deeds and glorify God on the day He visits us.*
—1 PETER 2:11–12

*Jesus said, "Go into the world and preach the good news
to all creation. Whoever believes and is baptized will be
saved, but whoever does not believe will be condemned.*
—MARK 16:15–16

ATHLETE

Every sport has extra periods to determine a winner when the game is tied at the end of the regulation time. Baseball goes into extra innings; basketball and football have overtimes; and golf has extra playoff holes—all to declare a winner. During these extra periods, the pressure to perform increases significantly, knowing that one mistake can result in defeat or that one quality play can produce a win. The ability to perform under pressure, focus, and be disciplined is never more relevant than during these extra periods. *One play and how you perform it can make you a winner or loser.* In some cases, it produces a legacy that follows you for the remainder of your life.

GAME OF LIFE

In the game of life, the closer we get to the end of life, the more we want to know what lies beyond death. When we get to the "overtime" of our lives, when extra innings may be needed to be successful in the game of life, what do we do? How do we find out what is beyond death? What assurances do we have that we played the game the way God intended? God loves us, and He has provided the answers in the Bible. *Accept Christ, make Him Savior and Lord of your life, and you have nothing to worry about beyond your earthly death.* Stand firm in your faith to the end, and God will bring you home to your reward, as promised in John 3:16.

God wants us with Him. He has shown us the way, the truth, and the life. Accept God's promise and experience paradise in heaven. Reject Christ and suffer the consequences. In the game of life, when you get down to your very last breath, the most important decision you will have made is *whether you accepted or rejected Jesus Christ. Your salvation depends on it.* It is never too late to accept Christ. The criminal on the cross next to Jesus found this out when he professed his faith in Christ and was promised paradise.

NOTES, COMMENTS, OR REFLECTIONS

*Paul said, "I want to know Christ and the power of His resurrection
and the fellowship of sharing in His sufferings, becoming like
Him in His death, and so, somehow, to attain to the resurrection
from the dead. I want to forget what is behind and straining
toward what is ahead. I press on toward the goal, to win the prize
for which God has called me heavenward in Christ Jesus.*
—PHILIPPIANS 3:10–11, 13

*Let those who love the Lord hate evil, for He guards the lives of
His faithful ones and delivers them from the hand of the wicked.*
—PSALM 97:10

ATHLETE

Athletes and teams set goals. Setting goals serves as motivation to succeed and sets a standard for performance. Young high school athletes set goals to improve, to get better. College athletes seek to improve their habits through practice and repetition to win games and get into playoffs. Professional athletes set goals to win, learn from their mistakes, improve weaknesses, and build on strengths to obtain monetary goals. Teams set goals to practice harder, win games, and win championships. Coaches set goals for themselves. They seek to find leaders and performers who can help the team reach those goals. You cannot participate successfully in competitive sports without setting goals. Once those goals have been met, new and higher goals need to be set. Setting goals, putting in the time to achieve those goals, and achieving those goals are a fundamental part of every sport, athlete, and team.

GAME OF LIFE

In the game of life, Christians must also set goals. The apostle Paul clearly set forth his goals in scripture. *Once you have accepted Christ as Savior and are committed by faith to make Him the Lord of your life, the next goal should be to strengthen your relationship with the Lord.* To do this, you need to make God part of your daily life through prayer, Bible reading, and daily devotionals. It's important to know and understand God's expectations for His followers. His commandments are clearly defined in the Bible. He wants us to love Him and our neighbors. He wants us to share the gospel. He wants us to put our faith into action. He wants us to be more like Jesus: kind, forgiving, humble, loving, righteous, and good. And when we fail, He wants us to repent, confess our failures, and learn from our wrongs; when we do so, He extends His grace and mercy to those who do. *God never stops loving you.*

NOTES, COMMENTS, OR REFLECTIONS

62
OUT OF YOUR LEAGUE

Do not be afraid of those who kill the
body but cannot kill the soul.
—MATTHEW 10:28

For many are invited, but few are chosen.
—MATTHEW 22:14

John the Baptist said, "After me will come one more
powerful than I, the thongs of whose sandals I am not
worthy to stoop down and untie. I baptize you with
water, but He will baptize you with the Holy Spirit.
—MARK 1:7–8

ATHLETE

"Out of your league" is a sports metaphor referring to someone or some team that is considered too difficult or good for you or your team. With respect to athletes, it has a negative connotation, reflecting a lack of respect for one's abilities or accomplishments. It suggests that the athlete or team doesn't have the ability to compete with a team that is out of their league. We all know, however, that the underdog will use that motivation to compete harder to pull off the upset and outperform the team that is supposedly superior. Every sport has numerous athletes and teams defeating other athletes and teams who have superior talent and accomplishments. This is what makes sports so compelling.

GAME OF LIFE

In the game of life, Christians will come under attack for having beliefs, adhering to biblical values, and not accepting worldly values. Christians are never out of their league when standing firm on their positions because the Lord has their back. He will sustain them, support their endeavors, and reassure them regarding their values and the godly positions they take.

God will see that you are always within your league. He will provide you with His protection, grace, and comfort. *When you stand firm for God's righteousness, your performance will not only be valuable and trustworthy, but it will put you in a league of your own and make you one of His most valuable players.*

NOTES, COMMENTS, OR REFLECTIONS

63
LITTLE LEAGUE WORLD SERIES

Train a child in the way he should go, and when he is old, he will not turn from it.
—**PROVERBS 22:6**

How great is the love the Father has lavished on us, that we should be called children of God, and that is what we are.
—**1 JOHN 3:1**

Let the little children come to me, and do not hinder them, for the kingdom of God belongs to such as these. I tell you the truth, anyone who will not receive the Kingdom of God like a little child will never enter it.
—**MARK 10:13–14**

ATHLETE

One of the most popular sports all over the world is Little League baseball or softball. The most popular sporting event may well be the Little League World Series. Teams from around the world gather in the summer and compete for this title. It is an American game but truly an international event. Why is it so well received? Why is it so popular? Because it embodies two of the greatest treasures on earth and in every country—love and children. Parents love watching their children play a game they love and learn about teamwork. Children play the sport because of their love for it. Little League coaches love teaching and mentoring these youngsters for the pure sake of enjoyment. No one loses in the Little League World Series—they are all winners.

GAME OF LIFE

The game of life embraces the culture created by children. Christians recognize that second only to the gift of Jesus Christ is the gift of children. Any person who has witnessed a child being born has witnessed God's miracle. The innocence of a child is pure joy. It is something to be nurtured, replicated, and duplicated. Children present us with a lifetime of memories. Children are a blessing from God. Christians must stand for them, protect them, provide for them, teach them, nurture them, and provide them with access to Jesus Christ. Without a doubt, that is God's will. *We must all stand for protecting the life of the fetus, nurturing children in the Christian faith, and protecting their innocence.*

NOTES, COMMENTS, OR REFLECTIONS

Trust in the Lord with all your heart and lean not on your own understanding; in all your ways acknowledge Him, and He will make your paths straight.
—PROVERBS 3:5–6

May the Lord our God be with us as He was with our fathers; may He never leave us or forsake us. May He turn our Hearts to Him, to walk in all His ways and to keep the commands, decrees and regulations He gave our fathers.
—1 KINGS 8:57–58

The good man brings God things out of the good stored-up in his heart; and the evil man brings evil things out of the evil stored-up in his heart. For out of the overflow of his heart, his mouth speaks.
—LUKE: 6:45

ATHLETE

When discussing morale, former US president Dwight Eisenhower said, "The will to win, the fighting heart, are the hallmarks of the coach and player." Likewise, they are the characteristics of successful people in all walks of life. In sports, the heart serves as a metaphor for commitment, desire, effort, and a team-first attitude. Coaches teach their teams to play with heart. They want players who are compassionate about their efforts and the team's success. Players who play till the whistle blows or the horn sounds, ending the game, play with heart. *You've got to have heart to find sustained success in sports competitions.*

GAME OF LIFE

In the game of life, we recognize that the heart controls our very being. It not only pumps blood to keep us alive but also controls and supports the brain, the words we speak, and the actions we take. God wants us to have a clean mind and a pure heart. Goodness, like evil, is rooted in the heart. By having a good heart, we reject evil. Having a heart for the Lord produces the attributes He wants His followers to have. These include love, grace, forgiveness, wisdom, understanding, counsel, fortitude, knowledge, piety, respect, and fear of the Lord. Commitment to the Lord with a good and faithful heart results in "goodness and love" following us all the days of our lives and allows us to spend eternity with Him (Psalm 23).

NOTES, COMMENTS, OR REFLECTIONS

And God will wipe away every tear from their eyes.
—REVELATION 7:17

The Lord upholds all those who fall and lifts-up all who are bowed down.
—PSALM 145:14

It is better to take refuge in the Lord than to trust in man.
—PSALM 118:8

ATHLETE

Anyone who has ever participated in sports has experienced hard times. Losing streaks, batting slumps, missed free throws, three-putt greens, injuries, and rebellion all contribute to hard times. Hard times, when confronted, can be motivation for building character. There is a belief in sports that "tough times never last, but tough people do." There is another famous quote that "winners never quit, and quitters never win." When facing hard times, athletes need to come together, make the team bond stronger, and rely on teammates, coaches, and family to help them get through those times. *Practice, repetition, faith, confidence, and trust will sustain you during hard times. Never give up. Never give in. Fight hard to the very end.*

GAME OF LIFE

In the game of life, Christians know that relying on the Lord during hard times will bring peace, comfort, and strength. It will also eventually result in victory over hard times. God may use adversity and hard times to strengthen your relationship with Him. God will wipe away your tears, work for your good, and uphold you if you believe and have faith in Him. Here are some rules to live by when experiencing hard times:

1. Take refuge in the Lord.
2. Let it go. Don't let a bad yesterday ruin a good day.
3. Ignore your critics. Rely on the Lord to empower you.
4. Stay calm and exercise patience because it may take some time for you to figure out hard times with God's help.
5. Don't compare yourself to others. Just be who God made you to be. God will bring you joy, but it is up to you to find happiness.
6. Smile. Life is short, so enjoy it while it lasts. There is one critical decision to make in life—acceptance of Jesus Christ as Lord and Savior. Failure to do so will result in hard times for eternity.

NOTES, COMMENTS, OR REFLECTIONS

66
PRIORITIES

But seek first His Kingdom and His righteousness,
and all things will be given to you as well.
—MATTHEW 6:33

Search me, O God, and know my heart; test me and
know my anxious thoughts. See if there is any offensive
way in me and lead me in the way of everlasting.
—PSALM 139:23–24

Jesus answered, "It is written, man does not live on bread alone,
but on every word that comes from the mouth of God."
—MATTHEW 4:4

ATHLETE

Priorities are essential for athletes. In secondary schools, parents frequently set priorities with good grades and good report cards taking precedence over sports and are a condition for athletic participation. In college and professional sports, the emphasis is on physical conditioning, mental toughness, a team-first mentality, and winning. As athletes get older, some distractions can destroy an athlete's priorities. Money, fame, material possessions, sex, pride, jealousy, and drugs can make it difficult for the athlete to reach his or her goals or team goals. It's up to each athlete to determine his or her priorities and then exercise the discipline necessary to achieve success in the athletic arena.

GAME OF LIFE

In the game of life, all individuals will face some of the same distractions as athletes. Society will tempt you to seek things that are destructive, such as sex, alcohol, money, drugs, and material possessions. *God recognizes that many desires and temptations are normal. After all, the devil presented Jesus with temptations.* God wants His followers to do what Jesus did, reject ungodly temptations, and first seek His kingdom. Seeking God's will over yours will result in God's blessings. Make seeking God's will your priority. *Start your morning prayers with a request that God's will be done in your life.* He will make sure you are blessed beyond measure.

NOTES, COMMENTS, OR REFLECTIONS

Jesus said, "I tell you the truth, one of you will betray me—one who is eating with me. But woe to that man who betrays the Son of Man! It would be better for him had he not been born."
—MARK 14:18, 20

Judas, who betrayed Jesus, saw that Jesus was condemned; he was seized with remorse and returned the thirty silver coins to the chief priest and elders ... Judas went away and hanged himself.
—MATTHEW 27:3, 5

He who is not with Me is against Me, and he who does not gather with Me scatters. And so I tell you, every sin and blasphemy against me will not be forgiven. Anyone who speaks a word against the Son of Man will be forgiven, but anyone who speaks against the Holy Spirit will not be forgiven, either in this age or in the age to come.
—MATTHEW 12:30–32

ATHLETE

The word *hardball* references an athlete, team, or opponent who acts ruthlessly and uncompromisingly toward competitors. Teams that run up scores as well as athletes and teams who beat a weaker opponent to submission are said to be playing hardball. Frequently, teams who are the recipient of hardball tactics will use the initial defeat as a motivating factor in a rematch. The object of sports is to compete, give your best effort, and win the game. The spirit of sports is to respect your opponent, respect the game, and compete fairly and with integrity. Athletes should be humble in victory and gracious in defeat.

GAME OF LIFE

Judas Iscariot, one of Christ's disciples, attempted to play hardball with Jesus by identifying Jesus to those who sought to persecute Him in exchange for thirty silver coins. His actions were ruthless and uncompromising, leading to the death of Jesus. He suffered the consequences of playing hardball. In the game of life, we are regularly confronted by those who challenge our Christian faith. Yet we remain loyal to our Creator through our reverence for Christ. God protects His followers from those who attempt to play hardball against them. Remember, our loving God doesn't send people to hell; rather, this is a choice nonbelievers make that causes them to suffer the consequences.

NOTES, COMMENTS, OR REFLECTIONS

The Beatitudes:

Blessed are the poor in spirit for theirs is the Kingdom of Heaven. Blessed are those who mourn for they will be comforted; blessed are the meek for they will inherit the earth; blessed are those who hunger and thirst for righteousness, for they will be filled; blessed are the merciful for they will be shown mercy; blessed are the pure in heart, for they will see God; blessed are the peacemakers for they will be called Sons of God; blessed are those persecuted because of righteousness, for theirs is the Kingdom of Heaven; blessed are you when people insult you, persecute you, falsely say evil things against you because of me … Rejoice and be glad, because great is your reward in Heaven.
—MATTHEW 5:3–12

ATHLETE

In sports, a wild card can refer to an unknown or unpredictable factor in the competition. It can also refer to teams with a win-loss record that qualifies that team for the playoffs, even though their record isn't the best in their league. Four wild card teams have won the MLB World Series; seven wild card teams have won the NFL Super Bowl; four wild card teams have won NBA championships. In hockey, the USA team, composed of amateurs, defeated a Russian pro team to win the gold medal in the historic "Miracle on Ice" Olympics. Wild cards prevail when the athlete or team is playing its best when the playoffs begin, when players believe in the team and trust each other, when players develop heart and mental toughness, and when players share the ball. The favorites are regularly upset by the wild card.

GAME OF LIFE

Jesus's Beatitudes tell us that in the game of life, the favorites don't always win; the powerful don't always rule. Wild cards can be winners. How so? They do so by being humble and thankful, by sharing blessings, by forgiving, by turning from sin and toward God, by loving one another, and by loving God. Being rich, powerful, famous, or successful guarantees nothing in the game of life. God wants the rich, powerful, famous, and successful to use their blessings as a platform to share with those who are less fortunate. God wants His people to spread the gospel and point others to the cross of salvation. In the game of life, be a wild card. Do the unexpected and claim your trophy in heaven. A wild card who does these things becomes the "salt of the earth," the "light of the world."

NOTES, COMMENTS, OR REFLECTIONS

*These people honor Me with their lips, but their
hearts are far from me. They worship me in vain;
their teachings are but rules taught by men.*
—MATTHEW 15:8–9

*Jesus said, "Go into the world and preach the good news
to all creation. Whoever believes and is baptized will be
saved, but whoever does not believe will be condemned."*
—MARK 16:15–16

*Jesus said, "Whoever loses his life for Me
and for the gospel will save it."*
—MARK 8:35

ATHLETE

If you are on the sidelines, you aren't actually in the game. A player or
athlete who stays on the sidelines, while important, isn't an important part
of playing the game. On the sidelines, you are an observer. This doesn't
mean you cannot become an integral part of the game when presented
with the playing opportunity. Therefore, you must prepare yourself to
play, you must learn from your sideline observance, and you must perform
when given the opportunity to enter the game.

GAME OF LIFE

In the game of life, many people are willing to talk the talk but unwilling to walk the walk. They verbally claim they are actively participating in the game, but their actions say otherwise. God knows the sincerity of your heart. He wants your actions to support your language. God looks at your heart. God looks at your activity. He seeks to determine whether your conduct is consistent with your rhetoric. Ask yourself daily, "Am I in the game, or am I just all talk?" *To play in God's game, you must be in the arena and back up your talk with your actions.* Don't be a hypocrite. Get in the game and make the most of your opportunity.

NOTES, COMMENTS, OR REFLECTIONS

He heals the brokenhearted and binds up their wounds.
—PSALM 147:3

I can do everything through Him who gives me strength.
—PHILIPPIANS 4:13

ATHLETE

Injuries are part of sports. Competition creates effort. Effort creates contact. Contact creates injury—some self-inflicted, some inflicted by the opponent. You cannot play sports without suffering some type of injury during your playing career. Even the best-conditioned athletes experience devastating injuries. Don't let your injuries define you. Don't allow your disappointment to lead you to depression. Athletes use the rehabilitation process to get bigger, faster, stronger, and, as motivation to come back, better than ever. *Take the time during rehabilitation to understand what you need to do to get back in the arena, be a better teammate, and improve your athletic performance.*

GAME OF LIFE

In the game of life, you will experience many injuries, setbacks, losses, and harm. Divorces, death, finances, diseases, illnesses, and accidents result in physical, mental, and emotional injuries that can prove difficult to overcome. Fear not, for the Lord heals the brokenhearted. He restores your strength when you ask for His help. Whatever you ask for in prayer, ask in faith and believe it will be answered. God will respond. God gives power to those who believe. Those who wait for the Lord will find their strength renewed. They shall run and not be weary; they shall walk and not faint (Isaiah 40:28–31). *There is no injury (physical, mental, emotional, or spiritual) that God cannot overcome and get you through to a better place.*

NOTES, COMMENTS, OR REFLECTIONS

71
LOVE, TRUST, AND FAITH

*Those who know Your name will trust in You, for You,
Lord, have never forsaken those who seek You.*
—PSALM 9:10

*For the Lord watches over the way of the righteous,
but the way of the wicked will parish.*
—PSALM 1:6

*Let love and faithfulness never leave you; bind them around your neck;
write them on the tablets of your hearts. Then you will win favor and
a good name in the sight of God and man. Trust in the Lord with all
your heart and lean not on your own understanding, but in all your
ways acknowledge Him, and He will make your path straight.*
—PROVERBS 3:3–6

ATHLETE

*Many congruent emotions are fundamental to sports and life. Love, trust, and
faith are perhaps the three most important ones.* Athletes must love their sport
to endure the training and effort it takes to be successful. They must love
and trust their teammates. They must embrace competition. They must
trust their coaches and the system the coaches are teaching. Athletes
must have faith in their training, coaching, and teammates. Without love,
trust, and faith, neither athletes nor teams will excel, win, and compete
for championships.

GAME OF LIFE

Both the Old Testament and New Testament lay forth the foundations for living as a Christian. Loving Christ, trusting God, having faith in God's word, and having faith that the Holy Spirit will guide you and protect you are the keys to winning in the game of life. God's two greatest commandments are to love Him with all your heart, soul, mind, and strength; and to love others as we love ourselves (Matthew 22:37–40). Trusting God to deliver on His promises is motivation for all, especially those in doubt.

Atheists and agnostics challenge Christians for loving, trusting, and having faith in something or someone they have never seen. If, however, they spent time reading the Bible, meditating on God's words, and praying, they would see God every day. He is there when you see acts of love, when you see miracles being performed, and when He answers prayers by granting specific bequests. He was there on the cross to save all mankind forever. *Love, trust, and faith—don't leave home without them, for they provide the assurances that the Holy Trinity is real and life changing.*

NOTES, COMMENTS, OR SUGGESTIONS

72
ABUNDANCE
OF RICHES

*It is easier for a camel to go through the eye of a needle
than for a rich man to enter the Kingdom of God.*
—MARK 10:23–24

*The apostle Paul said, "Command those who are rich in this
present world not to be arrogant, not to put their hope in wealth,
which is so uncertain, but to put their Hope in God, who richly
provides us with everything for our enjoyment. Command them
to do good deeds, and to be generous and willing to share."*
—1 TIMOTHY 6:17–18

ATHLETE

Riches are abundant in professional sports. Those riches have trickled
down into college sports through the name, image, likeness (NIL) rulings,
allowing college athletes to be compensated for the use of their NIL. Team
owners of professional teams are frequently billionaires. Most professional
teams will have several millionaires. Star college athletes in big-time
college programs will receive NIL compensation that will make them
rich by most standards. Failure to manage their rich blessing has resulted
in some very successful athletes being broke within a few years after
retiring. Others manage their money in such a manner to set up charitable
foundations that provide for those in need.

GAME OF LIFE

In the game of life, Christians understand that it's not a sin to have an abundance of riches. Many high-profile ministers have an abundance of riches. The difficulty for rich people entering the kingdom of heaven was Jesus's way of saying that rich people shouldn't rely on their wealth or themselves in seeking immortality; rather, they must rely on the same beliefs that those of lesser means rely on—trust or faith in Jesus Christ as Lord and Savior.

Christians trust God to provide life abundantly as He has promised for those who seek Him. God put us here to share our blessings and make life better for others. In Proverbs, the Bible makes it clear that *God values hard work*. He appreciates those who are frugal and manage their riches wisely (Proverbs 13:11). The Bible makes it clear that God wants us to share our abundance of riches with those in need. On judgment day, God will ask each of us what we did with the blessings He bestowed on us to make life better for others. What will be your response?

NOTES, COMMENTS, OR REFLECTIONS

73
A WHOLE NEW BALL GAME

Moses said, "I have set before you life and death, blessings and curses. Now choose life, so that you and your children may live and that you may love the Lord, your God, listen to his voice and hold fast to Him. For the Lord is your life and he will give you many years in the promised land.
—DEUTERONOMY 30:17

Jesus said, "Come, you who are blessed by my Father; take your inheritance, the Kingdom prepared for you since the creation of the world. For I was hungry, and you gave me something to eat. I was thirsty, and you gave me something to drink. I was a stranger, and you invited me in. I needed clothes, and you clothed me. I was sick, and you looked after me. I was in prison, and you came to visit.
—MATTHEW 25:34–36

ATHLETE

When an athlete or team encounters a completely different situation, one that is difficult or one they know little about, it is said that such a situation presents a "whole new ball game." The expression comes from baseball, where it signifies a complete turn of events. For example, a team leads the game almost the entire way, only to lose the lead in late innings. It requires the athlete and/or team to make a choice—adapt, adjust, and change. Otherwise, defeat is inevitable.

GAME OF LIFE

God chose to come to earth in the form of a human—Jesus Christ. He walked among the people. He performed miracles. He healed the sick, raised the dead, and fed the hungry. He lived for approximately thirty-three years before being crucified. He came to serve, not to condemn. He came to save sinners. He came to fulfill the prophecy of the Old Testament. He came to save men and women from themselves. He took on the sins of the world for eternity for those who believed and accepted Him as Lord and Savior.

Jesus presented the world with a whole new ball game. God gave us Jesus so that no matter how far we had fallen in life, no matter the lateness of the game, Jesus was there to save us and give us a whole new ball game. If we accept Him, we win and take our place in the Promised Land, heaven. If we don't accept Him, we lose the game of life and suffer the consequences. Choose life. Choose Jesus.

NOTES, COMMENTS, OR REFLECTIONS

*My son, preserve sound judgment and discernment; do not
let them out of your sight; they will be life for you.*
—**PROVERBS 3:21–22**

*For wisdom is more precious than rubies, and nothing
you desire can compare with wisdom.*
—**PROVERBS 8:11**

*By wisdom a house is built and through understanding,
it is established; through knowledge its rooms are
filled, with rare and beautiful treasures.*
—**PROVERBS 24:3–4**

ATHLETE

Wisdom is one's knowledge of what is true, what is real. Athletes obtain wisdom from their experiences. An athlete who possesses wisdom will generally exercise good judgment. Unfortunately, most wisdom comes from the athlete's failures or mistakes. Knowing what to do and when to do it is what wisdom is all about. Success builds confidence. Wisdom builds success. Many professional athletes leave the sport, knowing when to retire; that is wisdom. Many professional athletes know how to handle their finances and leave their sport in good financial condition; that is wisdom. Those who lack wisdom find themselves broke after a few years in retirement. *Wisdom is more important to longevity than money.*

GAME OF LIFE

In the *game of life, wisdom is developed through successes and failures.*

Successes and failures are inevitable in everyone's life. How you handle success and failure will determine the quality of your life. *If you want wisdom, then develop a personal relationship with Jesus Christ.* Individuals who spend time in prayer, Bible reading, meditation on God's word, and participation in Christian activities will be the recipient of God's wisdom.

God will guide you, protect you, provide for you, and support you emotionally and spiritually. He will free you from sin and guilt. He will bring you peace, forgiveness, love, grace, and mercy; and you will feel the wiser for His blessings. God possesses all the wisdom there is, and He will gladly share it with those who seek Him. *Seek God. Find wisdom.*

NOTES, COMMENTS, OR REFLECTIONS

75
TIME AND CHANCE

The race is not to the swift, or the battle to the strong, nor does food come to the wise or wealth to the brilliant or favor to the learned; but time and chance happen to all.
—ECCLESIASTES 9:11

Yet, a time is coming and has now come when the true worshipers will worship the Father in spirit and truth, for they are the kind of worshippers the Father seeks. God is spirit and his worshippers must worship in spirit and in truth.
—JOHN 4:23–24

Show me, O Lord, my life's end and the number of my days; let me know how fleeting is my life. You have made days a mere hard breath: the span of my years is nothing before you. Each man's life is but a breath.
—PSALM 39:4–5

ATHLETE

Every sport involves time and chance. Being in the right place at the right time is what time and chance are all about. During your playing career, you will be given a chance to make a difference. Score the winning touchdown, make the winning basket or free throw, hit a dramatic home run, or sink a long putt to win a tournament. These are all examples of time and chance in sports. If you make the most of the opportunity, you will be hailed as a hero.

Failure in those circumstances will bring criticism. but failure used as motivation will lead to success. Just remember Babe Ruth, the greatest home run hitter of all time. He struck out 1,330 times. Michael Jordon, the greatest basketball player, missed twenty-six game-winning shots and missed more than nine thousand shots in his playing career. Time and chance don't always produce success, but in the power of failure, there is motivation to improve, work harder and smarter, and be a better player and teammate.

GAME OF LIFE

The game of life will present everyone with opportunities to take advantage of the time and circumstances in which he or she finds himself or herself. Being in the right place at the right time will occur in every facet of your life—education, marriage, career choices, business opportunities, investing, parenthood, friendships, and your religious faith (or lack thereof). The Bible reminds us that time is fleeting. *God will provide us with time and a chance to do good and righteous things.* There will be a time to get to know Jesus as Savior, to study and learn biblical values, and to share love and encouragement with those in need. The most important time-and-chance decision you will ever make is whether to accept Christ as Savior. You must get this decision right. After death, there is no second chance. *When God calls you, answer Him.*

NOTES, COMMENTS, OR REFLECTIONS

Therefore, go and make disciples of all nations, baptizing them in the name of the Father and of the Son and of the Holy Spirit.
—MATTHEW 28:19

And hope does not disappoint us, because God has poured out His love into our hearts by the Holy Spirit, whom He has given us … Christ died for the ungodly.
—ROMANS 5:5–6

Jesus said, "I and the Father are one … why then do you accuse me of blasphemy because I said, 'I am God's Son'? Do not believe me unless I do what my Father does. But if I do it, even though you do not believe Me, believe the miracles, that you may know and understand that the Father is in Me, and I am in the Father."
—JOHN 10:29, 36–38

ATHLETE

The hat trick is a sports metaphor for the scoring of three goals by a single player in one game. It originated in the English sport of cricket. It occurred when a bowler (pitcher) would retire three batters in a row with three consecutive pitchers, a rare feat. As a reward, the bowler (pitcher) received a hat. The term was made famous by the sport of hockey. A hockey player who scores three goals in one game is said to accomplish the hat trick. He or she would be rewarded with fans throwing hats onto the ice.

After a time, other sports have their own definition of a hat trick. In basketball, it means one player having double-digit points, rebounds, and assists in one game. In soccer, a perfect hat trick is when a player scores three separate goals—one with the right foot, one with the left foot, and one with the head. In baseball, the hat thick occurs when one player hits three home runs in one game. In life, the metaphor has been used to recognize the accomplishments of a single individual, such as an actor winning three Oscars. So, young athletes and young adults, go perform your hat trick.

GAME OF LIFE

In the game of life, the hat trick is found in the doctrine of the Holy Trinity. Jesus recognized the Holy Trinity when He instructed His followers to go and baptize nations in the name of the Father, the Son, and the Holy Spirit (Matthew 28:19). The Holy Trinity takes on three different forms, all of whom are unified in God Almighty. God, our heavenly Father, created all things in the world and the universe. It is He who provides us with our souls. God recognizes the sinful nature of man or woman. He loved us so much that He came to earth as Jesus Christ. He walked among the living, performing miracles only God could perform to prove Jesus was, indeed, God in the flesh. Jesus was both human and divine. His purpose was to provide us with His teachings, to show us a righteous path to follow, and ultimately to serve as a sacrifice for our sins, thus reconciling imperfect sinners with a perfect God. Those who accept Christ as Savior will receive the Holy Spirit, who, in turn, will guide them and their consciences on their life's journey. For us Christians, accepting the Holy Trinity as one God is the hat trick by which God will reward us with our heavenly crowns.

NOTES, COMMENTS, OR REFLECTIONS

I, the Lord, do not change.
—MALACHI 3:6

Jesus said, "I tell you the truth, unless you
change and become like little children, you
will never enter the Kingdom of Heaven.
—MATTHEW 18:3

The apostle Paul said, "What you heard from me, keep as
a pattern of sound teaching, with faith and love in Christ
Jesus. Guard the good deposit that was entrusted to you—
guard it with the help of the Holy Spirit who lives in us.
—2 TIMOTHY 1:13

ATHLETE

The one constant that permeates all sports is change. Athletes change positions, teams, bodies, and mindsets. Teams change ownership, players, and coaches. Golfers change equipment, their swings, their putting stroke, and their golf balls. In sports, change is inevitable and is usually done to make things better. Change can be difficult because it invariably involves resisting well-established behavioral patterns. Change isn't always popular and is seldom easy. It's a recognition, however, that something is wrong and needs to be fixed. Change must be done cautiously and with direction, purpose, and objectives.

GAME OF LIFE

In the game of life, one constant never changes—the Father, the Son, and the Holy Spirit. *God is the same—from the beginning of time until infinity.* God hasn't changed and won't change. Men and women must change to win victory in Christ. The apostle Paul is a perfect example of the type of change needed in the game of life. He went throughout the region, persecuting Christians until God confronted him. His experience with God led him to embrace Christ, surrender his will to God's, and convert people to the Christian faith. He wrote a significant portion of the New Testament.

The change God envisions, indeed commands, is found in children—innocence, pure love, trust, sincerity, faith, unconditional belief, acceptance, and loyalty. Habits are difficult to change. Life patterns are difficult to change. The most difficult thing to change is one's heart. The change God wants is for us to accept Christ as Savior, receive the Holy Spirit. and surrender our wills to God's will. He won't fail you. He will support and prosper you.

NOTES, COMMENTS, OR REFLECTIONS

*For although they knew God, they neither glorified Him as
God nor gave Thanks to Him, but their thinking became
futile, and their foolish hearts were darkened.*
—ROMANS 1:21

*They mouth empty, boastful words and, by appealing to the lustful
desires of sinful human nature, they entice people who are just escaping
from those who live in error. They promise freedom, while they themselves
are slaves of depravity—for a man is a slave to whatever masters him.*
—2 PETER 2:18–19

*Do not allow what you consider good to be spoken of as evil.
The Kingdom of God is not a matter of eating and drinking,
but of righteousness, peace and joy in the Holy Spirit.*
—ROMANS 14:16–17

*In you, O Lord, I have taken refuge; let me never be
put to shame, deliver me in your righteousness.*
—PSALM 31:1

ATHLETE

The term "free rein" is a metaphor that originated in horse racing. The
rider holds the reins loosely and controls the horse, allowing it to move
freely at its own pace and in the desired direction. Free rein is often
referred to as giving the athlete or player the freedom to do whatever he
or she chooses. It references the ability of the athlete to have freedom,
unrestrained activity, and unlimited play. Free rein is frequently seen in

the Hail Mary pass in football, the base stealing in baseball, the attempt to drive a par four in golf, and a shooter being given the green light to shoot at will. Circumstances and the athlete's ability determine when to exercise free rein.

GAME OF LIFE

In the game of life, God gives all people a free will (free rein), which allows them to move freely, choose their pace, and move in the chosen direction. You have the freedom to choose what you believe and how you respond to your beliefs. There are consequences to exercising one's free will. God makes it clear that He loves you. He wants you to accept His promise of eternal life through Jesus Christ. He wants you to live a good, righteous life and to make life better for others. He has promised that those who accept Him will have a life of peace, joy, love, and prosperity. He wants you to be with Him forever at the end of your life. In the game of life, Christians exercise their free will (free rein) to be part of God's kingdom on earth and in heaven. How will you choose to exercise your free rein?

NOTES, COMMENTS, OR REFLECTIONS

GLASS JAW

For all have sinned and fallen short of the glory of God.
—ROMANS 3:23

Who will rescue me from this body of death? Thanks be to God, through Jesus Christ, our Lord.
—ROMANS 7:25

No one who is born of God will continue to sin because God's seed remains in him; he cannot go on sinning, because he has been born of God.
—1 JOHN 3:9

ATHLETE

Athletes and teams are said to have a glass jaw when they are vulnerable to an opponent's knockout punch. In almost every sport, coaches and scouts spend hours reviewing game videos and looking for their opponents' glass jaw. They also review video to determine their own glass jaw. Game plans are drawn around an opponent's glass jaw and his or her team's weaknesses. Weaknesses are overcome by disguising the glass jaw, focusing on strengthening it, and practicing to produce better athletic performance.

GAME OF LIFE

In the game of life, every individual has a glass jaw. The glass jaw is sin. We have all sinned. We will all continue to sin, even after we accept Christ.

Sin leads to death and destruction of the soul. God recognized this, and because of His great love, He determined a way in which all sin could be forgiven and reconciled to a perfect God.

Jesus said, "I am the Truth, the Way, the Life" (John 14:6). He is the Truth because He is exactly who He said He was—the Son of God. He is the Way to the forgiveness of sin and reconciliation with God. He is the Life because He provides His followers not only with prosperity during their earthly lives but also with eternal life upon their death. Sin doesn't have to weigh you down. Ask God to help you get rid of the glass jaw in your life—and He will.

NOTES, COMMENTS, OR REFLECTIONS

80
MENTAL
TOUGHNESS

But he who stands firm to the end will be saved.
—MATTHEW 10:22

*Love comes from God … God is love … No one has
ever seen God, but if we love one another, God lives
in us, and His love is made complete in us.*
—1 JOHN 4:7–8, 12

*Keep yourself in God's Love as you wait for the mercy
of our Lord Jesus Christ to bring you eternal life.*
—JUDE 1:21

ATHLETE

Mental toughness is required to play and participate in sports. You will experience many adversities while playing sports. Sports events are about competition and winning, and in the process, much effort is expended, much frustration is encountered, and losses are part of the sports competition. We have all heard the reference that "it matters not how many times you have been knocked down, but rather how many times you have gotten back up." You must be mentally tough to recover and perform. Nothing quiets your critics like getting off the mat and turning in a positive performance.

Mental toughness refers to an athlete's ability to persist in the face of challenges, mistakes, and failures. Mental toughness is built by articulating and operating within a core set of values, by having clear direction and a sense of purpose, by building trust and value in the contributions of teammates, by managing your weaknesses, and by building on your strengths.

GAME OF LIFE

Christians must be mentally tough. Critics and friends will belittle you, make fun of you, ridicule you, and exclude you. They will attempt to embarrass you with your beliefs. But Christians have something those friends and critics don't have: God owns their hearts and has their backs. God's support and encouragement make them mentally strong.

Christians care more about what God thinks than about what their friends and critics think. God will never forsake you. He will never allow you to suffer more than your ability allows you to withstand. Proverbs 19:23 notes, "The fear of the Lord leads to life so that one rests content, untouched by trouble." In the game of life, Christians develop mental toughness with God's help and love.

NOTES, COMMENTS, OR REFLECTIONS

81

MAKING THE CUT

God will give to each person according to what he has done. To those who by persistence in doing good seek glory, honor and immortality, He will give eternal life. But for those who are self-seeking and who reject truth and follow evil, there will be wrath and anger. There will be trouble and distress for every human being who declares evil but glory, honor and peace for everyone who does good.
—**ROMANS 2:6–10**

If anyone's name was not found written in the book of life, he was thrown into the lake of fire.
—**REVELATION 20:15**

For many are invited, but few are chosen.
—**MATTHEW 22:14**

ATHLETE

For athletes competing in team sports, the first objective is to make the cut (i.e., be chosen as a member of the team). Making the cut ensures you of making the team. Demonstrated, consistent performance keeps you on the team. Producing positive results under pressure makes you a team leader. Quality and sustained winning performances can make you a star. Not all-star athletes make the cut initially. The greatest basketball player ever, Michael Jordon, was cut from his high school team as a sophomore. Tom Brady, quarterback, and the GOAT of professional football, was a sixth-round draft choice with questionable odds of surviving the cut. Both used these perceived failures as motivation to become the best in their sport.

Don't let a failure to make the cut define you as an athlete. You define yourself by how you react to not making the cut.

GAME OF LIFE

Now listen to what follows. Read it, grasp it, believe it, and live it. In the game of life, there is only one decision that will define whether you make the cut. Have you accepted Jesus Christ as your Lord and Savior?

The answer to that question determines where you will spend eternity. Put your faith and trust in the redemptive work Jesus Christ performed through His death and resurrection. Put your name on the team roster (Book of Life) and get into the game of life.

NOTES, COMMENTS, OR REFLECTIONS

82
SPORTS CHAMPIONSHIPS

*But thanks be to God, He gives us the victory
through our Lord Jesus Christ.*
—1 CORINTHIANS 15:57

*Do you know that in a race all the runners run, but only one
receives the prize? So run in such a way as to get the prize.*
—1 CORINTHIANS 9:24

*What good will it be for a man if he gains the
whole world, yet forfeits his soul?*
—MATTHEW 16:26

ATHLETE

Playing for championships is the most valuable objective in sports. To be identified as a champion, as the best in your sport, is a major accomplishment. Championships are won as a result of talent, hard work, practice, sacrifice, trust, discipline, selflessness, quality play, and coaching. Trophies are won, rings are adorned by players, fame follows players, and coaches lead championship teams. Being a champion carries a lifelong feeling that for a brief period, you are recognized as the very best, and in some cases, you earn a spot in sports immortality.

GAME OF LIFE

In the game of life, Christians receive something far greater than a trophy or a ring when they choose to be part of God's championship team. They receive real immortality in paradise. They also receive a "peace which surpasses all understanding" and guards your heart and mind through Christ Jesus (Philippians 4:6). Christians live without fear. Christians live with unsurpassed love. Christians become champions forever. This status cannot be taken from you; you don't have to defend it; you didn't earn it since it is a gift from the Lord, paid for by His sacrifice. Claim your victory in the game of life. Receive your coveted prize.

NOTES, COMMENTS, OR REFLECTIONS

Whoever wants to become great among you must be your servant, and whoever wants to be first must be a slave of all. For even the Son of Man did not come to be served, but to serve, and to give His life as a ransom for many.
—MARK 10:43–45

And this is the will of Him who sent me, that I shall lose none of all He has given me … For my Father's will is that everyone who looks to the Son and believes in Him shall have eternal life, and I will raise them up the last day.
—JOHN 6:39–40

Jesus said, "I give them eternal life and they shall never parish.; no one can snatch them out of my hand. My Father who has given them to me is greater than all; no one can snatch them out of my Father's hand. I and the Father are one."
—JOHN 10:28–29

ATHLETE

Athletes love praise and glory. Being selected to the Hall of Fame in their sport is the ultimate personal acknowledgment. It produces a sense of accomplishment, of self-worth, and allows the recipient to accept the reward for all the hard work that went into his or her career.

Athletes use this award as a platform on which to build a career once their playing days are over. They invariably thank their teammates, give credit to their coaches, and make expressions of gratitude to their families and friends. Fame is fleeting. It can leave you overnight like it did a Hall of Fame football player accused of murdering his wife and her friend. Wealth has been lost, and Hall of Fame careers have been tarnished by divorce, scandal, and bankruptcies.

GAME OF LIFE

In the game of life, every person who accepts Christ as Lord and Savior becomes a member of God's Hall of Fame. Being a Christian provides a platform for sharing the gospel of the New Testament. In God's Hall of Fame, you are immortal. Accept Christ, and you will never be removed from His Hall of Fame. Jesus tells us that once we are saved, we have eternal security (John 6:39–40). Jesus acknowledges in John 10:28–29 that once Christ is accepted, no one can remove the person from His grasp. God's Hall of Fame is open to all who accept and believe.

NOTES, COMMENTS, OR REFLECTIONS

Everyone who believes that Jesus is the Christ is born of God,
and everyone who loves the Father loves the Child as well.
—1 JOHN 5:1

I ask that we love one another. And this is love: that we
walk in obedience to His commands. As you have heard from
the beginning, His command is that you walk in love.
—2 JOHN 1:5–6

Keep yourselves in God's love as you wait for the mercy of
our Lord Jesus Christ to bring you to eternal life.
—JUDE 1:21

ATHLETE

"Love the game, and it will love you back" is a prevalent quote in sports. Its origin is attributed to a former NBA player. How does the game love you back? In professional sports, love of the game is frequently seen in highly compensating the players, making them rich and secure for life. In college sports, love of the game provides feelings derived from successful participation (including NIL) compensation. But the purest form of love paid back by the game is found in youth and high school sports and extends to college and professional athletes.

The euphoric feeling of love for the game that goes with participation is unsurpassed. Most athletes will tell you that this feeling is what drives them, motivates them, and makes playing the game worthwhile. Winning, participating, sharing, accomplishing, and bonding on a team are all forms of love the game gives back. The GOAT of basketball, Michael Jordan, talked about his love of the game. He said to play every game as if it were your last. Find your refuge in playing the game, and if you love the game, nobody can take that away from you. He recognized that the intense pain, coupled with the intense joy and satisfaction of playing the game, reflects the greatest respect and love of the game.

GAME OF LIFE

Every man and woman of faith understands the concept of love of the game. God is love, and when you love God with all your heart, mind, and soul, you will feel the greatest love that exists—the love of God. He never stops loving. Once you feel God's love, you must surrender your will to His. Once you accept the love Christ showed you on the cross and feel the love God has for you, then all the Lord requires is that you do what is right, love mercy and grace, and live humbly with the Lord (Micah 6:8).

NOTES, COMMENTS, OR REFLECTIONS

For everyone born of God overcomes the world. This is the victory that has overcome the world ... Who is it that overcomes the world? Only He who believes that Jesus is the Son of God.
—1 JOHN 5:4–5

For wide is the gate and broad is the road that leads to destruction, and many enter through it. But small is the gate and narrow the road that leads to life, and only a few find it.
—MATTHEW 7:13–14

But thanks be to God: He gives us the victory through our Lord Jesus Christ.
—1 CORINTHIANS 15:57

ATHLETE

From the first introduction into sport competitions, athletes are trained mentally and physically to pursue victories. Victories win championships. Teams are built to win. Athletes are trained to win. The ability to overcome adversity and injuries produces victories. Victories represent the "mother's milk" of sports. Victories extend careers. Victories create individual wealth. Victories bring fame. If victories weren't important, there would be no need to keep score. Winning never gets old, especially when done according to the rules and fair sportsmanship.

GAME OF LIFE

In the game of life, we set many goals related to education, careers, marriage, children, health, and retirement. As we achieve those goals, we claim victory and re-set new goals. *The one victory every person should seek to obtain is eternal life in heaven with the Lord and his or her loved ones.* There is no victory greater in life than the victory won through the life, death, and resurrection of Jesus Christ. The victory is there for all to claim. Words alone, however, won't achieve this victory.

God looks at your heart. He looks at your actions. He wants us to live lives by a faith that reflects our love of Christ. In the game of life, many obstacles will be placed in your path, such as alcohol, drugs, sex, immorality, lying, cheating, stealing, gossiping, pride, jealousy, and greed. They will constantly be thrown at you. By faith, God will grant you the strength, wisdom, and discipline needed to claim victory over these obstacles. Knowing Christ as Savior is the greatest victory.

NOTES, COMMENTS, OR REFLECTIONS

Therefore, there is now no condemnation for
those who are in Christ Jesus.
—ROMANS 8:1

Just as man is destined to die once, and after that to face
judgment, so Christ was sacrificed to take away the sins
of many people, and he will appear a second time, but to
bring salvation to those who are waiting for Him.
—HEBREWS 9:27–28

Do not judge, or you too will be judged. For in the same
way you judge others, you will be judged, and with the
measure you use, it will be measured to you.
—MATTHEW 7:1–2

ATHLETE

As an athlete, you will be *judged* on many different issues. Judgments will come from coaches, parents, fans, fellow athletes, and the news media, among others. Your performance will be judged. Your effort will be judged. Your results will be judged. It is important for athletes to understand whose judgment is important. Fans will criticize you, win or lose. Coaches will judge your effort based on the outcome. Your teammates will judge you based on your contributions. Social media can be brutal in judging an athlete's performance.

The most important judgment, however, is the one you make of yourself. Judging yourself can result in significant improvement. You must be honest when judging yourself. You must learn from the mistakes you make. An honest self-judgment will lead you to readily acknowledge the need for improvement. *Don't let others define you. Define yourself.*

GAME OF LIFE

In the game of life, you will be subjected to judgments every day. Spouses, children, employers, friends, and coworkers will often be quick to judge you, even without knowing all the circumstances. *God clearly wants us to refrain from judging others. Instead, He prefers that we pray for them, offer support to them, and extend our love, grace, and mercy to them as He has done to us.* Be positive because life is too short to continually see life negatively. Always remember that the most important judgment you should be concerned about is the one God places on your salvation.

NOTES, COMMENTS, OR REFLECTIONS

87

GAME, SET, MATCH

I press on toward the goal to win the prize for which
God has called me heavenward in Christ Jesus.
—PHILIPPIANS 3:14

Everyone who competes in the games goes into strict training.
They do it to get a crown that will not last; but we do it to get a
crown that will last forever. Therefore, I do not run like a man
running aimlessly; I do not fight the man beating the air. No,
I beat my body and make it slave so that after I have preached
to others, I myself will not be disqualified for the prize.
—1 CORINTHIANS 9:25–27

ATHLETE

In tennis, you play a game. When you win a certain number of games, you win the set. When you win the majority of the sets, you win the match. At the conclusion, the referee announces the conclusion by saying, "Game, set, match." It is an expression that means the competition has reached a conclusion. Volleyball is scored similarly. "Game, set, match" is frequently used in other sports competitions as a metaphor reflecting that one opponent has beaten the other. It is used in the business world as a term to reflect that the competition or opposition has been defeated.

GAME OF LIFE

Life is a lot like a tennis match. You are confronted with daily challenges (games). In the game of life, the goal is to meet and defeat those challenges.

Even if you are successful, there will be new challenges facing you the next day. It is a process that continues throughout life. Sin is alluring, and it won't go away simply because you have accepted Christ as Savior. While all sin is forgiven of those who accept Christ, the allure of sin doesn't stop. You will continue to face sinful challenges. Having accepted Christ as Savior, however, puts you in a position to declare victory over sin (set) and seek His strength to help you resist sinful temptations. *Make Christ the Lord of your life, and you will defeat sin and win the "match."*

NOTES, COMMENTS, OR REFLECTIONS

88

STAND BY YOU

*Put on the full armor of God so that you can take
a stand against the devil's schemes.*
—EPHESIANS 6:11

Do not fear, I will help you.
—ISAIAH 41:13

He will wipe every tear from their eyes.
—REVELATION 21:4

The Lord will fight for you.
—EXODUS 14:14

*Be strong and courageous … for the
Lord your God goes with you.*
—DEUTERONOMY 31:6

ATHLETE

Team sports at any level and in every sport create a bonding experience among teammates that can last a lifetime. Teammates bond because they expend so much energy and passion, and they do so together. The blood, sweat, and tears that go into training, practicing, participating, winning, and losing create a lifetime of shared experiences. *Good teammates stand by you, win or lose.* They have your back. They understand the "thrill of victory and the agony of defeat." One of the most emotional experiences in sports is watching teammates rally around athletes who make a play that results in defeat. Good teammates always stand by you.

GAME OF LIFE

In the game of life, you will have no better teammates than those Christians who stand by you in good times and bad. Jesus stood by you on the cross, and He isn't about to let you go. Neither Jesus nor your Christian friends will abandon you in time of need. They will stand by you. When you have done all you can but that isn't enough, they will *stand by you*. When you get emotional and depressed, they will wipe away your tears. When necessary, they will fight your fight, hold you tight, and not let go. Come join the team in the game of life.

NOTES, COMMENTS, OR REFLECTIONS

89
THROWING IN
THE TOWEL

Let us not become weary in doing good, for at the proper
time we will reap a harvest if we do not give up.
—GALATIANS 6:9

For God did not give us a spirit of timidity, but a
spirit of power, of love and self-discipline.
—2 TIMOTHY 1:7

Have I not commanded you? BE strong and courageous.
Do not be afraid, do not be discouraged, for the Lord
your God will be with you wherever you go.
—JOSHUA 1:9

Jesus said, "My Father, if it is possible, may this cup be
taken from me. Yet not as I will, but as you will.
—MATTHEW 26:39

ATHLETE

Every athlete, team, player, and competitor faces that "throwing in the towel" moment, which is a sports metaphor for quitting in defeat. The term originates from boxing, where the boxer, facing certain defeat, throws a towel into the ring, signifying he or she is surrendering and conceding defeat. It's difficult for athletes and players to throw in the towel after expending so much time and sacrifice in preparing to play the game. Coaches use the impossible circumstances as a learning experience to win or learn from the defeat. Good athletes or players looking for greatness learn to play their hardest until the horn sounds, ending the game. There is shame in defeat only in quitting or throwing in the towel.

GAME OF LIFE

Jesus faced a "throwing in the towel" moment before His crucifixion when He asked God to take this cup of suffering and salvation from Him. And yet He knew that God's will had to be done, that He had to endure the pain, agony, and suffering, for He was taking the sins of the world on Himself. He knew God's will had to be done to complete God's promise of sending a Messiah to save the people.

In the game of life, you will face many situations that appear impossible to overcome, where defeat appears certain. But God is awesome, and if you refuse to throw in the towel, He will be there to support you in every conceivable circumstance. You should continue to seek God's will and assistance, especially in the face of certain defeat.

NOTES, COMMENTS, OR REFLECTIONS

*May the God who gives endurance and encouragement
give you a spirit of unity among yourselves as you follow
Christ Jesus, so that with one heart and one mouth you may
glorify the God and Father of our Lord Jesus Christ.*
—ROMANS 15:5–6

*Since Christ suffered in His body, arm yourselves also with the
same attitude, because he who has suffered in his body is done
with sin. As a result, he does not live the rest of his earthly life
for evil human desires, but rather for the will of God.*
—1 PETER 4:1–2

ATHLETE

A full-court press in basketball is the most aggressive, exhausting defense a team can play. For it to be effective, all players must know their roles. They must communicate with one another. They must endure and encourage one another. The players must come together as one unit, executing their roles and relying on teammates to do the same. They must play with one heartbeat and in complete unity. This turns defense into offense by creating turnovers. When done properly, the full-court press is beautiful to watch and effective in demoralizing the opponent.

GAME OF LIFE

In the game of life, Christians, having accepted Christ as Savior, must put on the full-court press, getting sin out of their lives. How do they do that?

By knowing Christ not only as Savior but also as Lord of their lives. What does that look like? Praying and seeking God's will over your own is the best place to begin. Seek God's will in your life through Bible reading, daily devotionals, and asking yourself, "WWJD. What would Jesus do?" Jesus resisted sin. He had no evil, sinful desires. He drew on His relationship with His heavenly Father.

Just as Christ suffered and defeated sin, so must Christians defeat the sin that is alluring to their hearts and minds. When you know Christ as Savior and Lord of your life, you put on the full-court press against sin and evil. Victory is yours in the game of life.

NOTES, COMMENTS, OR REFLECTIONS

BLOCKING AND TACKLING

Make every effort to add to your faith, goodness; and to goodness, knowledge; and to knowledge, self-control; and to self-control, perseverance; and to perseverance, Godliness; and to Godliness, brotherly kindness; and to brotherly kindness, Love.

—2 PETER 1:5–7

The world and it desires pass away, but the man who does the will of God lives forever.

—1 JOHN 2:17

To prepare God's people for works of service, so that the body of Christ may be built up until we all reach unity in the faith and in the knowledge of the Son of God and becomes mature, attaining to the whole measure of the fullness of Christ. Then we will no longer be infants ... Instead, speaking the truth in love, we will in all things grow-up into Him who is the Head, that is, Christ. From Him, the whole body ... grows and builds itself up in love, as each part does its work.

—EPHESIANS 4:12–16

ATHLETE

In football, the team that wins the game is usually the one that executes two fundamentals: blocking and tackling. The concept of blocking and tackling is a metaphor ("coach speak") for applying the fundamental basics to any situation. In every sport, executing the fundamental basics is necessary to win the competition. After a loss, you will hear the coach say,

"We have to get back to the basics." This requires a change in behavior, a better focus, a greater commitment, and a better understanding of the fundamentals and how to execute them.

GAME OF LIFE

In the game of life, the Lord tells us that if we are to resist sin, we must execute the fundamentals (i.e., blocking and tackling) by always returning to the basics. For Christians, the fundamentals are faith, goodness, knowledge, self-control, perseverance, godliness, kindness, truth, God's will, and love. We must block sin out of our lives, and we must tackle anyone who encourages us to succumb to our sinful nature. We must always pray for the sinner, for forgiveness and mercy for him or her. In the game of life, do your blocking and tackling by always knowing and practicing your fundamentals.

NOTES, COMMENTS, OR REFLECTIONS

92
HAIL MARY

An angel of the Lord appeared to Joseph in a dream and said, "Joseph, son of David, do not be afraid to take Mary home as your wife, because what is conceived in her is from the Holy Spirit. She will give birth to a son, and you are to give him the name Jesus, because He will save people from their sins.
—MATTHEW 1:20–21

The angel said to Mary, "do not be afraid, Mary, you have found favor with God. You will be with child and give birth to a son, and you are to give Him the name Jesus. He will be great and will be called the Son of the Most High. His kingdom will never end ... the one to be born will be called the Son of God ... For nothing is impossible with God.
—LUKE 1:30–32, 35, 37

ATHLETE

The Hail Mary is used as a sports metaphor to characterize a last-ditch effort to win a game with little chance of success. In football, it is a long pass at the end of the game in an attempt to score a touchdown and win the game. It is derived from the Catholic Hail Mary prayer for strength or help. Conventional wisdom implies that it would take a miracle for the play to be successful.

The term originated in 1975 when Dallas Cowboys quarterback Roger Staubach told the press that after throwing a fifty-yard touchdown pass to win a playoff game, he said a Hail Mary prayer for its completion. There have been hundreds of attempts at throwing a Hail Mary pass at the end of the game. Less than 10 percent have been successful.

GAME OF LIFE

In the game of life, the Hail Mary is a traditional Christian/Catholic prayer, praising Mary and petitioning her for help with sinners who appear to be a lost cause or with a dire situation that appears impossible to overcome. The prayer is usually said as follows: "Hail Mary, full of grace, the Lord is with thee; blessed art thou among women and blessed is the fruit of thy womb, Jesus. Holy Mary, Mother of God, pray for us sinners, now and at the hour of our death. Amen." Jesus was conceived by the Holy Spirit (which makes Him divine) and was born of the Virgin Mary (which makes Him human). The virgin birth, one of God's greatest miracles, assures us that with God, nothing is impossible. *God's greatest gift to all is salvation through Jesus Christ.*

NOTES, COMMENTS, OR REFLECTIONS

93
SUCCESS

May those who delight in my vindication shout for joy and
gladness; may they always say, '" The Lord be exalted,
who delights in the well-being of his servant."
—PSALM 35:27

The blessing of the Lord brings wealth;
and he adds no trouble to it.
—PROVERBS 10:22

Lord, grant us success!
—PSALM 118:25

ATHLETE

Success has different meanings in sports. It can mean winning the ultimate championship. It can mean winning your conference or prevailing over your rival. It can mean improving your performance from previous years. You can be successful even when you lose, since there has been one MVP in the Super Bowl who played for the losing team.

The best definition of success is measured by the goals you set at the beginning of your competition. Did you, as an athlete, reach the goals you set for yourself? Did the team reach the goals it set? Every athlete and sports organization should establish goals at the beginning of the season. The goals need to be specific, measurable, achievable, relevant, and within a specified time frame. Only then can you measure whether you were successful. The most important measure of team success is productivity.

GAME OF LIFE

In the game of life, three key elements lead to success:

1. Purpose: You must clearly understand your purpose and what it is you want to achieve. You need direction as to where you want to go with your life. Most important, however, is knowing why you want to achieve that goal. Understand the sacrifices you will need to make to reach your goals.
2. Growth: If you are to have a growth mindset, you must be willing to act, not talk. You must be able to learn from your mistakes and failures. Failure to the highly motivated leads to success.
3. Courage: In life, you will need to take risks. You will face obstacles and need the courage to take on challenges if you are to succeed. In the game of life, accept Christ as Savior, and He will be with you, help you, and support you in your journey to succeed. God wants you to succeed.

NOTES, COMMENTS, OR REFLECTIONS

*A new command I give you: Love one another. As I have
loved you, so you must love one another. By this all men will
know that you are my disciples, if you love one another.*
—JOHN 13:34–35

Love your enemies and pray for those who persecute you.
—MATTHEW 5:44

*If I have faith that can move mountains, but have not love, I am
nothing. If I give all I possess to the poor and surrender my body
to flames, but have not love, I gain nothing. Love is patient, love
is kind; it does not envy; it does not boast; it is not proud. It is not
rude. It is not self-seeking; it is not easily angered; it keeps no records
of wrong. Love does not delight in evil but rejoices with the truth. It
always protects, always trust, always hopes, always perseveres.*
—1 CORINTHIANS 13:5

*Whoever does not love does not know God because God is love. This
is how God showed His love among us: He sent His one and only
Son into the world that we might live through Him. This is love,
not that we loved Him, but that He loved us and sent His Son as
an atoning sacrifice for our sins. Since God so loved us, we ought
to love one another. No one has ever seen God, but if we love one
another, God lives in us, and His love is made complete in us.*
—1 JOHN 4:8–12

*Love never fails. These three remain: faith, hope
and love. But the greatest of these is love.*
—1 CORINTHIANS 13:8, 13

ATHLETE

Love is pervasive throughout sports. Fans love their teams and athletes. Coaches love their players. Teammates love each other. All love their families, friends, and fans. One of the greatest loves athletes and team members experience is love of the sport they play. The love usually begins at an early age when they participate in sports for fun. They fall in love with the sport and seek to extend playing it throughout high school, college, and in some cases, the pros. Athletes love to win, compete, sweat, and expend energy while playing the game. Playing a game for a living is fun. When you love what you do for a living, you will never work a day in your life.

GAME OF LIFE

In the game of life, love is the core value. God is love's architect. It is the foundation upon which all other virtues rest. You cannot win in the game of life without love. The entire premise of the Bible is God's love for the people He created. God loved the world even as He witnessed so much sin and evil. He came to earth in the form of a human being (Jesus Christ) and walked among us, teaching us about love and sacrifice. He came to serve and demonstrate His love. Because God so loved the people of the world, He gave His only begotten Son so whosoever believes in Him shall not perish but shall have eternal life (John 3:16). He wants us to love Him and others, even those we consider adversaries. Build your life around love. It is the foundation for a happy, blessed life. Once you feel the pure passion, devotion, and tenderness love generates, you will see God—and God is beautiful.

NOTES, COMMENTS, OR REFLECTIONS

*In Him we have redemption through His blood,
the forgiveness of sin, in accordance with the
riches of God's grace that He lavished on us
with all wisdom and understanding.*
—EPHESIANS 1:7–8

*It is because of God that you are in Christ Jesus,
who for us has become wisdom from God—that is,
our righteousness, holiness and redemption.*
—1 CORINTHIANS 1:30

*May the words of my mouth and the meditation of my heart
be pleasing in your sight, O Lord, my Redeemer.*
—PSALM 19:14

ATHLETE

Redemption (the act of regaining something in exchange for payment) is a concept seen frequently in sports. A sports hero or icon falls from grace by committing some act of degradation, thereby setting himself or herself up for redemption. Tiger Woods's infamous marital scandal and Michael Vick's dog-fighting scandal are examples of sports icons who had to seek redemption. Both succeeded through redemptive conduct. SMU's college football team was given the death penalty by the NCAA as a result of recruiting violations. The Houston Astros had their World Series championships tarnished by cheating scandals. Both organizations were able to redeem themselves and regain their status through redemptive actions. If you play sports long enough, there is a probability that you will perform some act requiring redemption. Here's how athletes and teams redeem themselves:

1. Own your failure.
2. Ask for help.
3. Take affirmative action.
4. Institute standards that will prevent a recurrence.
5. Do your job.
6. Learn from your failures.

GAME OF LIFE

In the game of life, sinners have a redeemer, Jesus Christ. The Bible is consistent in its declarations that Jesus Christ was born, lived, and died to redeem sinners. Sinners are redeemed through Christ's love, grace, and mercy as shown on the cross. Once the sinner has accepted Christ as Savior, his or her sin (past, present, and future) is forgiven. Once sinners are redeemed, God expects them to make a sincere, good-faith effort to own their sin, seek His help for forgiveness, and take actions to minimize their sinful conduct. The good news is that the Lord is only a prayer away from providing your redemption. Redemption is yours for the asking. Christ is our redeemer.

NOTES, COMMENTS, OR REFLECTIONS

We proclaim to you that we have seen and heard, so that you also may have fellowship with us, and our fellowship is with the Father and with His Son, Jesus Christ. We write this to make our joy complete.
—1 JOHN 1:3–5

God, who has called you into fellowship with His Son, Jesus Christ our Lord, is faithful.
—1 CORINTHIANS 1:9

But if we walk in the light, as He is in the light, we have fellowship with one another, and the blood of Jesus, His Son, purifies us from all sin.
—1 JOHN 1:5–7

ATHLETE

Long after athletic careers are ended, athletes and members of the team will miss the fellowship developed among themselves more than the game. Shared athletic experiences, be they wins or losses, have a way of strengthening the bond between participants.

You must be able to communicate to be successful in the athletic arena. You must know as much as possible about your teammates. Fellowship teaches the athlete how to communicate. Fellowship helps athletes to accept coaching and constructive criticism. Fellowship creates team unity. Teams with good fellowship win championships. Fellowship promotes honesty and integrity.

GAME OF LIFE

In the game of life, organizations such as the Fellowship of Christian Athletes (FCA) use athletics as a platform for delivering the message of Jesus Christ. Integrity, service, teamwork, and excellence are traits the FCA uses to lead coaches, players, and fans into a relationship with Jesus Christ. FCA is the largest on-campus Christian organization in the world. It was formed to bring athletes together to reveal the transforming power of Christ. FCA has received criticism from atheist and agnostic organizations for not being more inclusive. The FCA leadership is much more concerned about what God thinks of their efforts than about what the world thinks. They recognize the apostle Paul's words in 1 Colossians 3:10. "Whatever you do work at it with all your heart, as working for the Lord, not for man, since you know you will receive an inheritance from the Lord as a reward. It is the Lord Christ you are serving."

NOTES, COMMENTS, OR REFLECTIONS

In My Father's house are many mansions; if it were not so, I would have told you. I go to prepare a place for you. And if I go and prepare a place for you, I will come again and receive you to Myself, that where I am, there you may be also.
—JOHN 14:2–3

They will see His face, and His name will be on their foreheads. There will be no more night. They will not need the light of the sun, for the Lord God gives them light. And they will reign forever and ever.
—REVELATION 22:4–5

For the Kingdom of God is not a matter of eating and drinking but of righteousness, peace and joy in the Holy Spirit.
—ROMANS 14:17

ATHLETE

Heaven has been described as a place of supreme happiness. Sports heaven is used to describe arenas that conjure up glorious moments experienced by a sport or team that regularly plays there. Yankee Stadium has been described as "Homer Heaven" and as "The Cathedral of Baseball." The Masters Golf Tournament is played on the Augusta National Golf Course, which is beautiful and has been referred to as "Heaven on Earth." The course even has an "Amen Corner" (holes eleven through thirteen). Madison Square Garden, home to NBA and NHL teams, has been described as basketball's heaven. Referring to a sports arena as heaven is nothing more than a colloquial expression of a place where athletes and players find supreme happiness in playing their sport. For those who have lost loved ones, the baseball field in the movie *Field of Dreams* might be considered heavenly since it was a place where people went to be reunited with their deceased loved ones.

GAME OF LIFE

In the game of life, there is only one heaven, the one God has prepared for His people. As Christians grow older, they naturally wonder what heaven will be like. God tells us in 1 Corinthians 2:9 that there are no words to describe its beauty. There are, however, numerous people who have had a near-death experience (NDE), during which they have received a glimpse of heaven. The book *Imagine Heaven* by pastor John Burke chronicles those experiences—a fascinating book. Those who have experienced NDEs describe heaven as so beautiful that it will take our breath away. It produced such an amazing feeling that they didn't want to leave. They talk about the peace, joy, and happiness they experienced. Heaven is described exactly as God promised—a place so beautiful that words cannot describe it. Heaven is the paradise God promises to those who accept Christ as Savior. Do you want to go to heaven?

NOTES, COMMENTS, OR REFLECTIONS

98
CROSS TO BEAR

Jesus said, "And anyone who does not take his cross and follow me is not worthy of me.
—MATTHEW 10:38

If anyone would come after me, he must deny himself and take up his cross and follow me.
—MARK 8:34

For the message of the cross is foolishness to those who are perishing, but to us who are being saved it is the power of God.
—1 CORINTHIANS 1:18

ATHLETE

Every athlete will be confronted by a "cross to bear." This term generally refers to an unpleasant or difficult situation the athlete alone must deal with. Athletes will invariably have a weakness in their game. For basketball players, poor free throw shooting can be a cross to bear. In golf, missing short putts regularly is a cross to bear. In baseball, the inability to hit a curve ball can be a cross to bear. In football, a player's fumbling or throwing too many interceptions can be a cross to bear. In every sport, athletes need to recognize their weaknesses, practice and train to improve those weaknesses, and eliminate those crosses to bear.

In the game of life, we recognize that as human beings, we have weaknesses. Those weaknesses invariably manifest themselves in some form of sin. Our cross to bear can present a painful or unpleasant situation we would prefer not to confront, but we must since we cannot allow the cross we bear to become addictions that are sinful, destructive, and damaging to our lives or to our relationship with Christ. Accepting Christ as Savior provides us with the greatest support we can have in confronting and solving the crosses we bear.

God will help you, but you will need to ask Him, and you will need to have great faith that He will respond to your request. Put down your cross and follow Jesus. He will give you peace, joy, and the ability to handle and resolve the problems weighing you down. Praise God!

NOTES, COMMENTS, OR REFLECTIONS

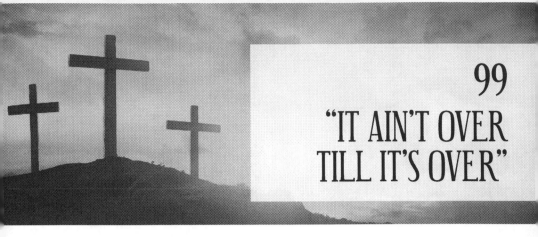

99

"IT AIN'T OVER TILL IT'S OVER"

Even now, declares the Lord, return to me with all your heart,
with fasting and weeping and mourning ... Return to the
Lord your God for he is gracious and compassionate.
—JOEL 2:12–13

I tell you the truth, today you will be with me in Paradise.
—LUKE 23:43

Father, forgive them for they do not know what they are doing.
—LUKE 23:34

I tell you, now is the time of God's favor, now is the day of salvation.
—2 CORINTHIANS 6:2

ATHLETE

Yogi Berra, the Yankee's Hall of Fame catcher, said, "It ain't over till it's over." Until the final horn sounds, ending the game, athletes or players should continue to give their best effort in hopes of pulling "victory from the jaws of defeat." This colloquy recognizes that the outcome of a situation shouldn't be taken for granted because circumstances can change. The perfect example of this is the NFL playoff game between the Buffalo Bills and the Kansas City Chiefs in 2022. Both teams scored several points in the last two minutes of the game to send it into overtime. The Bills scored with thirteen seconds left to play to take the lead. The Chiefs used the final thirteen seconds to get into field goal range. The Chiefs kicked a field goal as time expired, sending the game into overtime, when the Chiefs won. Every sports fan has witnessed numerous contests won during the last play of the game when it appeared the game was lost. *The message is simple. Never give up until the final play of the game because "it ain't over till it's over."*

GAME OF LIFE

In the game of life, your soul isn't lost until your life ends without you accepting Christ as Savior. No matter how late in life you come to accept Christ as Savior, you can be saved. On the day Christ was crucified, two criminals shared the same fate as Christ. Just before He died, one of the criminals acknowledged Christ for who He was and asked Christ to remember him. Jesus said to the criminal, "Today, you will be with me in Paradise." Clearly, salvation "ain't over till it's over." Salvation is yours if in faith you accept Christ as Savior. A deathbed confession of acceptance of Christ as Savior, made in good faith, is sufficient to obtain salvation. In the game of life, "it ain't over till it's over." Save your soul for eternity. Waiting until the last minute, however, deprives you of the prosperous life God wants to give you. When you feel in your heart that God is calling you, accept His call regardless of the timing.

NOTES, COMMENTS, OR REFLECTIONS

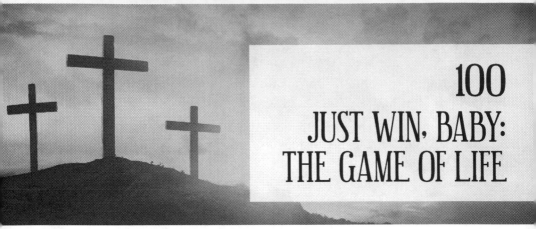

100

JUST WIN, BABY: THE GAME OF LIFE

The fruit of the righteous is a tree of life, and
he that winnneth souls is wise.
—**PROVERBS 11:30**

I tell you that there will be more rejoicing in Heaven
over one sinner who repents than over ninety-nine
righteous persons who do not need to repent.
—**LUKE 15:10**

For the Son of Man came to seek and to save what was lost.
—**LUKE 19:10**

And He saith unto them, come follow me, and
I will make you fishers of men.
—**MATTHEW 4:19**

ATHLETE

Two famous NFL coaches, Vince Lombardi and Al Davis, had famous quotes about winning. Lombardi said, "Winning isn't everything; it is the only thing." Davis said, "Just win, baby." Sports is about winning; otherwise, why keep score? Winning builds confidence. Winning produces rewards and special privileges. Winning builds cohesion and team spirit. Winning creates motivation. The more you win, the more you want to win.

There is, however, another side to winning, especially in youth sports. In youth sports, the emphasis should be on participating and achieving. In youth sports, winning can often be attributed to physiological differences (one team being older, stronger, bigger, or faster). Winning also makes for a more gracious loser. Not all teams are going to win every game. *Losing with honor and grace makes you a winner.*

GAME OF LIFE

There is only one way to win the game of life—by accepting Jesus Christ as Lord and Savior. Your reward is eternal life in heaven. You cannot earn your way into heaven. You cannot buy your way into heaven. You cannot earn the reward of heaven by being a good person. The most important decision you will make in your life is whether you have accepted Christ as the Savior and Lord of your life. It's never too late to make that decision if you are alive. The longer you wait to accept Christ as Savior, the more you are missing out on the richness and fullness of living a Christian life. God sees that His followers receive earthly rewards. Just win, baby, the game of life!

NOTES, COMMENTS, OR REFLECTIONS

Jesus said, "It is finished" and He bowed
His head and gave up His spirit.
—JOHN 19:30

The time has come for my departure. I have fought the good
fight. I have finished the race. I have kept the faith. Now there
is in store for me the crown of righteousness which the Lord,
the Righteous Judge, will award me on that day—and not only
me, but also to all who have longed for His appearing.
—2 TIMOTHY 4:6–8

What good is it for a man to gain the whole world,
and yet lose or forfeit his very self.
—LUKE 9:25

To the Athlete Playing the Game of Life and to All Young Adults:

In every game and sport, there comes a time when it is finished. The game is over. Someone wins, and someone loses. The outcome is certain when the game ends. Life is the same way. Life begins at conception. It ends at death. In between being born and dying is the period we refer to as "life." How we live our lives determines where we will spend eternity. Ask yourself these questions:

1.   Did I know and accept Jesus Christ as my Lord and Savior?
2.   Did I place my faith and trust in Him?
3.   Did I use His blessings to make life better for others?
4.   Did I serve Him as a giver, not a taker?
5.   Did I repent of my sins and seek God's forgiveness, grace, and mercy?

6. Did I treat others the way I wanted to be treated?
7. Did I seek and follow His will and forgive as I was forgiven?
8. Did I fear God and live as He instructed—with kindness, integrity, goodness, righteousness, and love?
9. Did I love the Lord with all my heart, soul, mind, and strength? And did I make the effort to love my neighbors as I love myself?
10. Did my conduct reflect my acceptance of Christ as Savior?

Your answers to these questions will determine whether you win or lose in the game of life. Praise God for the winners. For the losers, may God have mercy on their souls. In life, you will have wins and losses. In Jesus Christ, you will always have victory. Just Win Baby: The Game of Life.

NOTES, COMMENTS, OR REFLECTIONS

THE JUST WIN BABY: PRAYER FOR ATHLETES

Heavenly Father,

Thank You for the blessing of sports. Thank You for blessing me with the physical skills and mental toughness to be an athlete. Thank You for my coaches, teammates, and fans. Thank You for my competitors. Keep us all safe. Give us strength to compete and persevere, to play by the rules, and to be thankful for the opportunity playing sports presents. Let us be humble in victory; let us be gracious in defeat.

But most of all, let us conduct ourselves in a manner to bring honor, praise, and glory to our Lord and Savior, Jesus Christ. May Your will be done.

Thank You, Jesus, for Your love, mercy, and saving grace.

Amen.

BIBLIOGRAPHY

All scripture quotations, unless otherwise noted, are taken from New International Version – Life Application Study Bible, published by Tyndale House Publishers, Inc. and Zondervan Publishing House, copyright 1988, 1989, 1990, 1991, and used with permission. Scriptures are mostly quoted verbatim. Verses that have been paraphrased do not change either the meaning or intent of the verse.

Printed in the United States
by Baker & Taylor Publisher Services